Our Lady of H...
THE GRAPHIC NOVEL

The author/illustrator of this book wishes to remain anonymous.
The panels were colored by an illustrator who also wishes to remain anonymous.

ISBN-13: 978-0-9994520-0-4
ISBN-10: 0-9994520-0-2

Books published by The Deo Gratias Company are available at quantity discounts on bulk purchases for premium, educational, fund-raising, and special sales use. For details please call 888-962-9322.

THE
Deo Gratias
Company

DeoGratiasCo.com

Printed in The United States of America

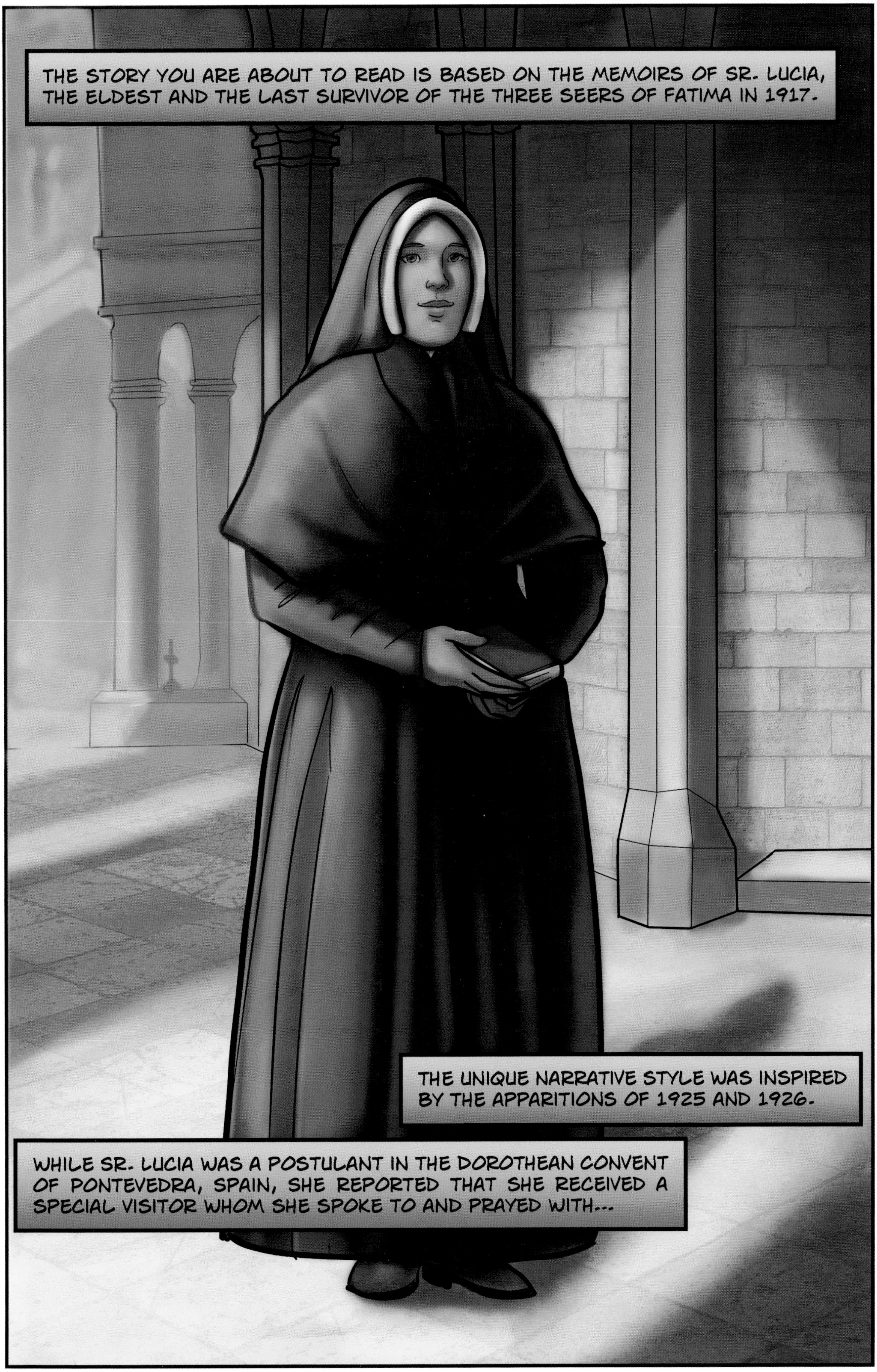
THE STORY YOU ARE ABOUT TO READ IS BASED ON THE MEMOIRS OF SR. LUCIA, THE ELDEST AND THE LAST SURVIVOR OF THE THREE SEERS OF FATIMA IN 1917.
THE UNIQUE NARRATIVE STYLE WAS INSPIRED BY THE APPARITIONS OF 1925 AND 1926.
WHILE SR. LUCIA WAS A POSTULANT IN THE DOROTHEAN CONVENT OF PONTEVEDRA, SPAIN, SHE REPORTED THAT SHE RECEIVED A SPECIAL VISITOR WHOM SHE SPOKE TO AND PRAYED WITH...

An Angel Story

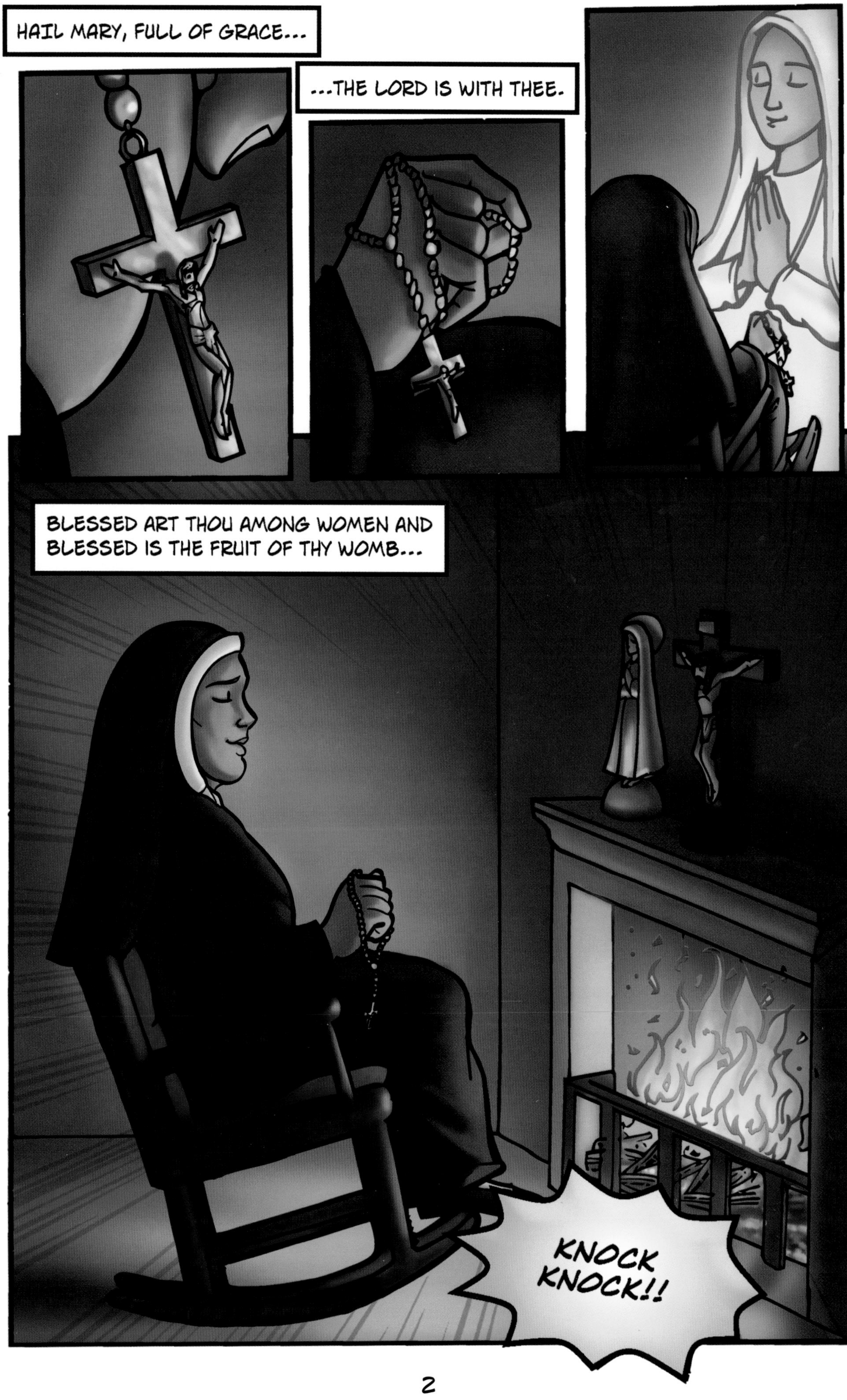
HAIL MARY, FULL OF GRACE...
...THE LORD IS WITH THEE.
BLESSED ART THOU AMONG WOMEN AND BLESSED IS THE FRUIT OF THY WOMB...
KNOCK KNOCK!!

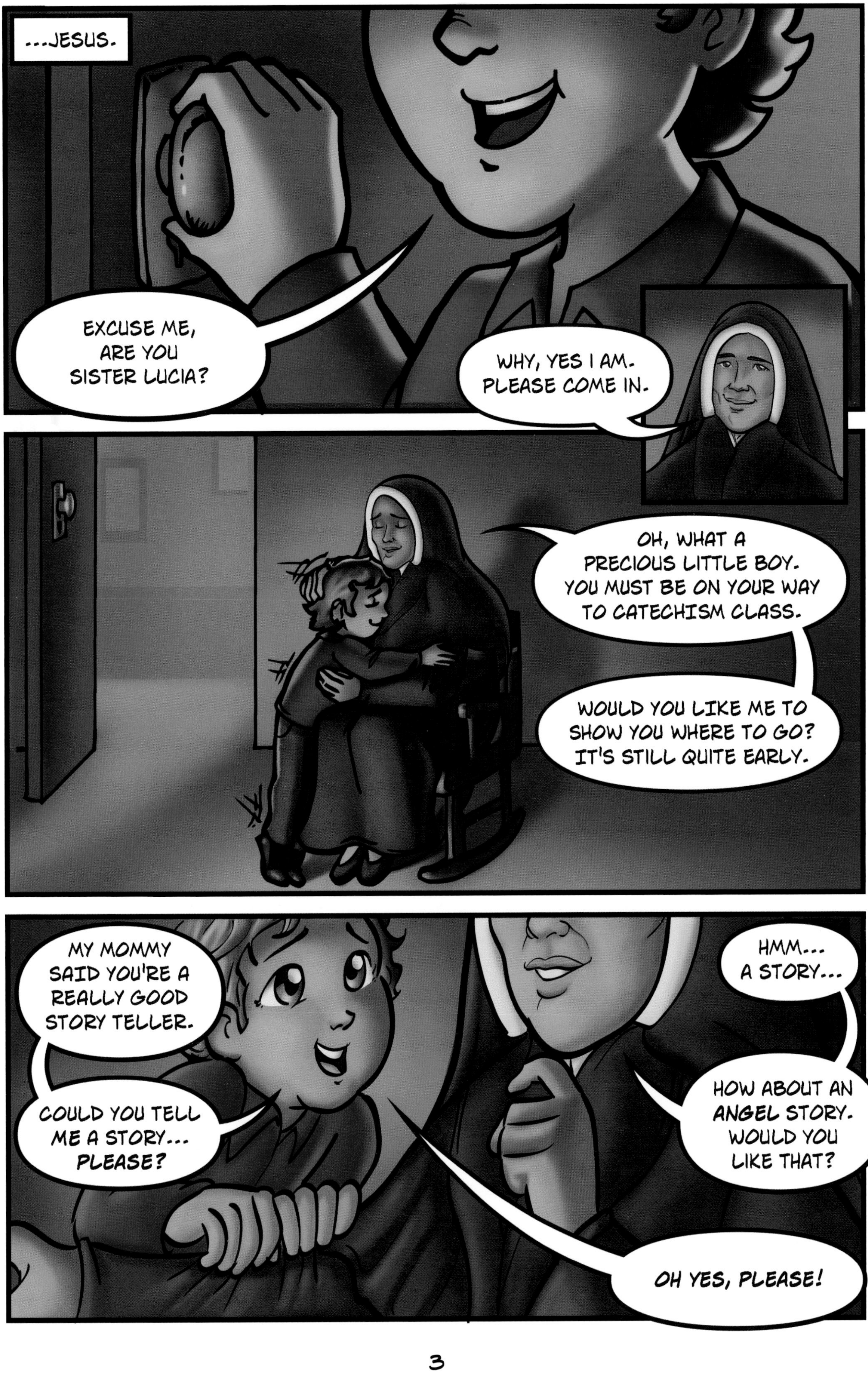
...JESUS.
EXCUSE ME, ARE YOU SISTER LUCIA?
WHY, YES I AM. PLEASE COME IN.
OH, WHAT A PRECIOUS LITTLE BOY. YOU MUST BE ON YOUR WAY TO CATECHISM CLASS.
WOULD YOU LIKE ME TO SHOW YOU WHERE TO GO? IT'S STILL QUITE EARLY.
MY MOMMY SAID YOU'RE A REALLY GOOD STORY TELLER.
COULD YOU TELL ME A STORY... PLEASE?
HMM... A STORY...
HOW ABOUT AN ANGEL STORY. WOULD YOU LIKE THAT?
OH YES, PLEASE!

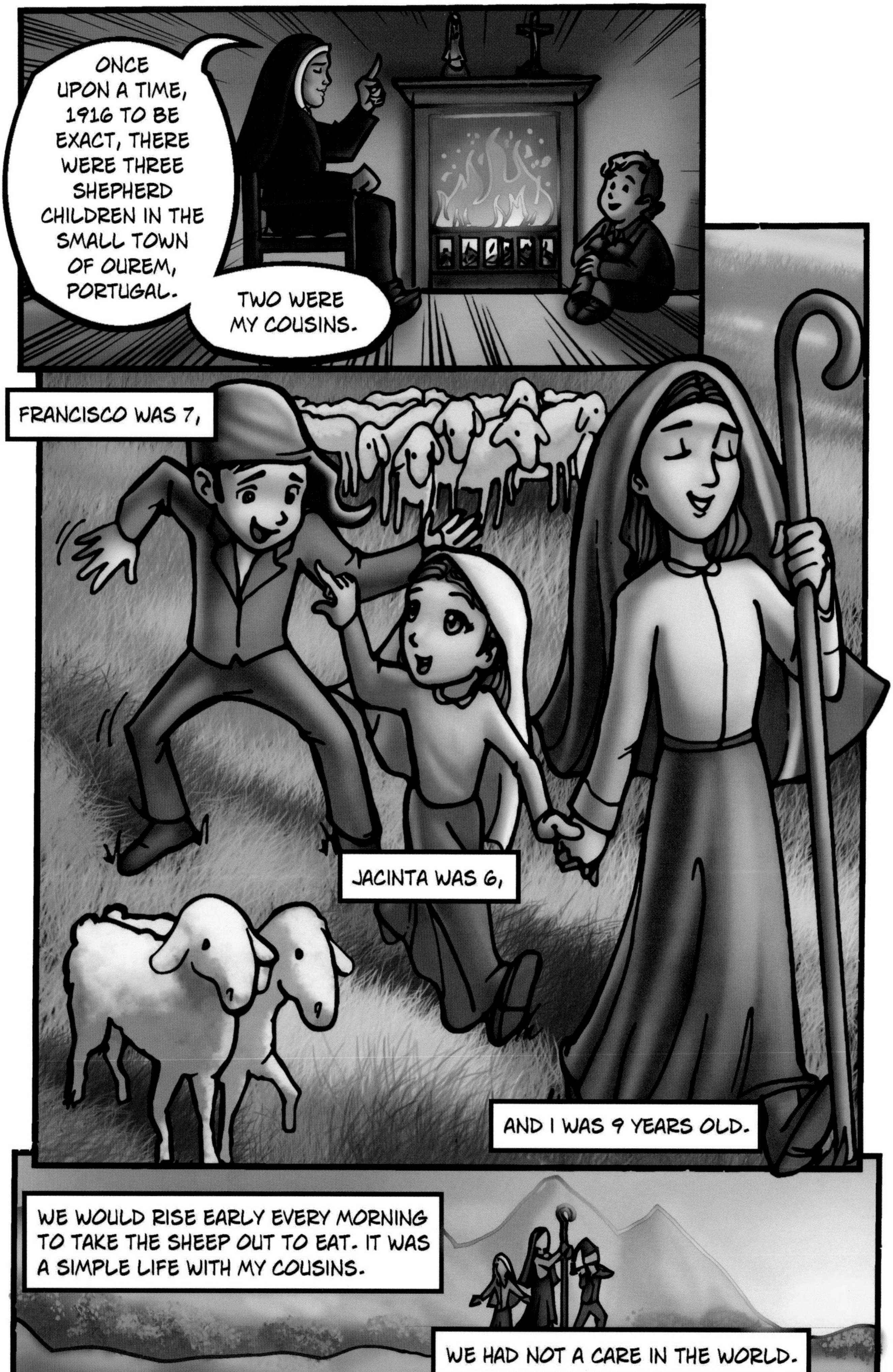
ONCE UPON A TIME, 1916 TO BE EXACT, THERE WERE THREE SHEPHERD CHILDREN IN THE SMALL TOWN OF OUREM, PORTUGAL.
TWO WERE MY COUSINS.
FRANCISCO WAS 7,
JACINTA WAS 6,
AND I WAS 9 YEARS OLD.
WE WOULD RISE EARLY EVERY MORNING TO TAKE THE SHEEP OUT TO EAT. IT WAS A SIMPLE LIFE WITH MY COUSINS.
WE HAD NOT A CARE IN THE WORLD.

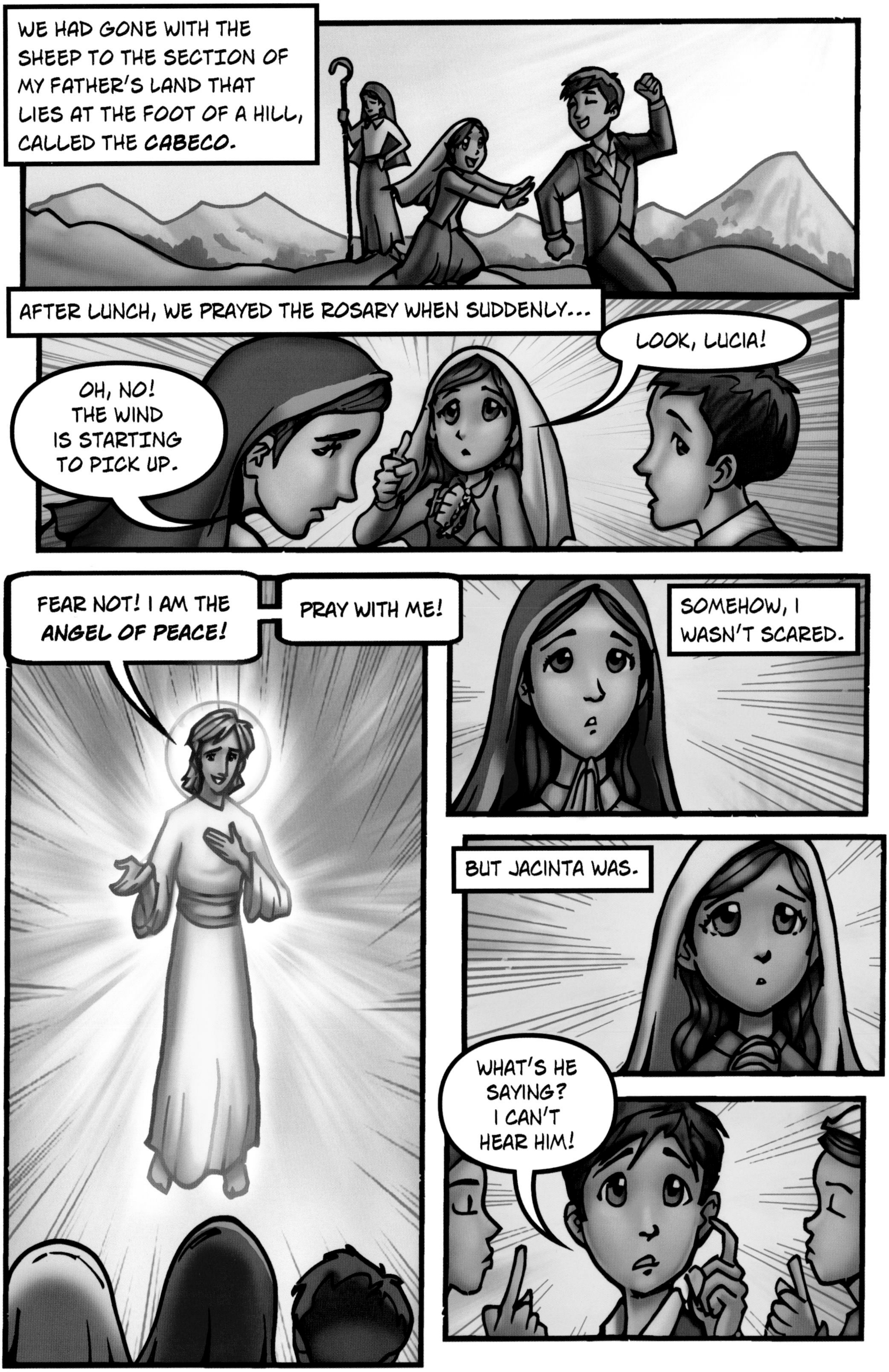
WE HAD GONE WITH THE SHEEP TO THE SECTION OF MY FATHER'S LAND THAT LIES AT THE FOOT OF A HILL, CALLED THE CABECO.
AFTER LUNCH, WE PRAYED THE ROSARY WHEN SUDDENLY...
OH, NO! THE WIND IS STARTING TO PICK UP.
LOOK, LUCIA!
FEAR NOT! I AM THE ANGEL OF PEACE!
PRAY WITH ME!
SOMEHOW, I WASN'T SCARED.
BUT JACINTA WAS.
WHAT'S HE SAYING? I CAN'T HEAR HIM!

THE ANGEL KNELT ON THE GROUND AND BOWED VERY LOW...

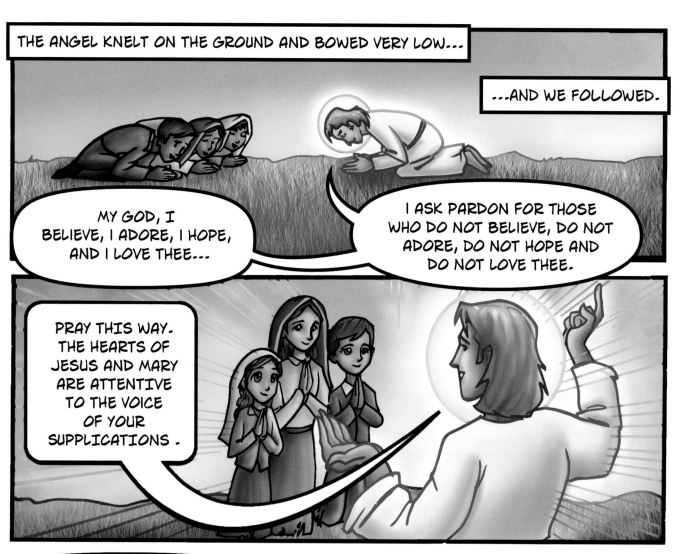

...AND WE FOLLOWED.

MY GOD, I BELIEVE, I ADORE, I HOPE, AND I LOVE THEE...

I ASK PARDON FOR THOSE WHO DO NOT BELIEVE, DO NOT ADORE, DO NOT HOPE AND DO NOT LOVE THEE.

PRAY THIS WAY. THE HEARTS OF JESUS AND MARY ARE ATTENTIVE TO THE VOICE OF YOUR SUPPLICATIONS.

SO...WHAT DID HE SAY?

HE SAID THAT JESUS AND MARY ARE LISTENING TO OUR PRAYERS!

THEN I'LL PRAY MORE ROSARIES!

I HOPE HE COMES AGAIN.

IN THE SUMMER OF 1916, HE DID RETURN.

WHAT ARE YOU DOING?

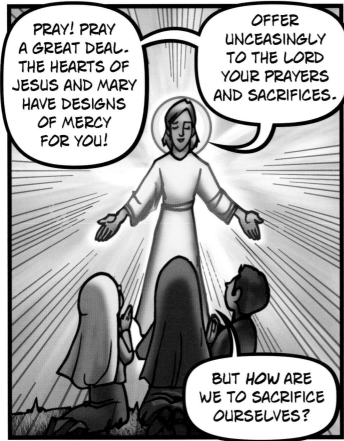

PRAY! PRAY A GREAT DEAL. THE HEARTS OF JESUS AND MARY HAVE DESIGNS OF MERCY FOR YOU!

OFFER UNCEASINGLY TO THE LORD YOUR PRAYERS AND SACRIFICES.

BUT *HOW* ARE WE TO SACRIFICE OURSELVES?

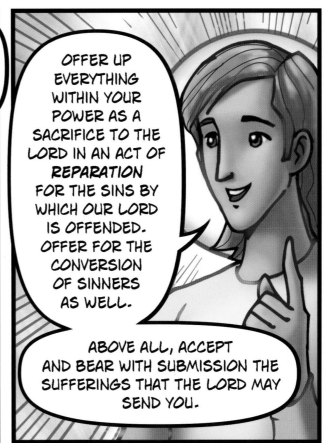

OFFER UP EVERYTHING WITHIN YOUR POWER AS A SACRIFICE TO THE LORD IN AN ACT OF *REPARATION* FOR THE SINS BY WHICH OUR LORD IS OFFENDED. OFFER FOR THE CONVERSION OF SINNERS AS WELL.

ABOVE ALL, ACCEPT AND BEAR WITH SUBMISSION THE SUFFERINGS THAT THE LORD MAY SEND YOU.

WHAT DID HE SAY *THIS* TIME?

I'LL TELL YOU TOMORROW, FRANCISCO.

THE CHALLENGE OF THE ANGEL TO MAKE *REPARATION* WAS SO INTENSE THAT I COULD HARDLY SPEAK. HOWEVER, THE NEXT DAY, I TOLD FRANCISCO EVERYTHING.

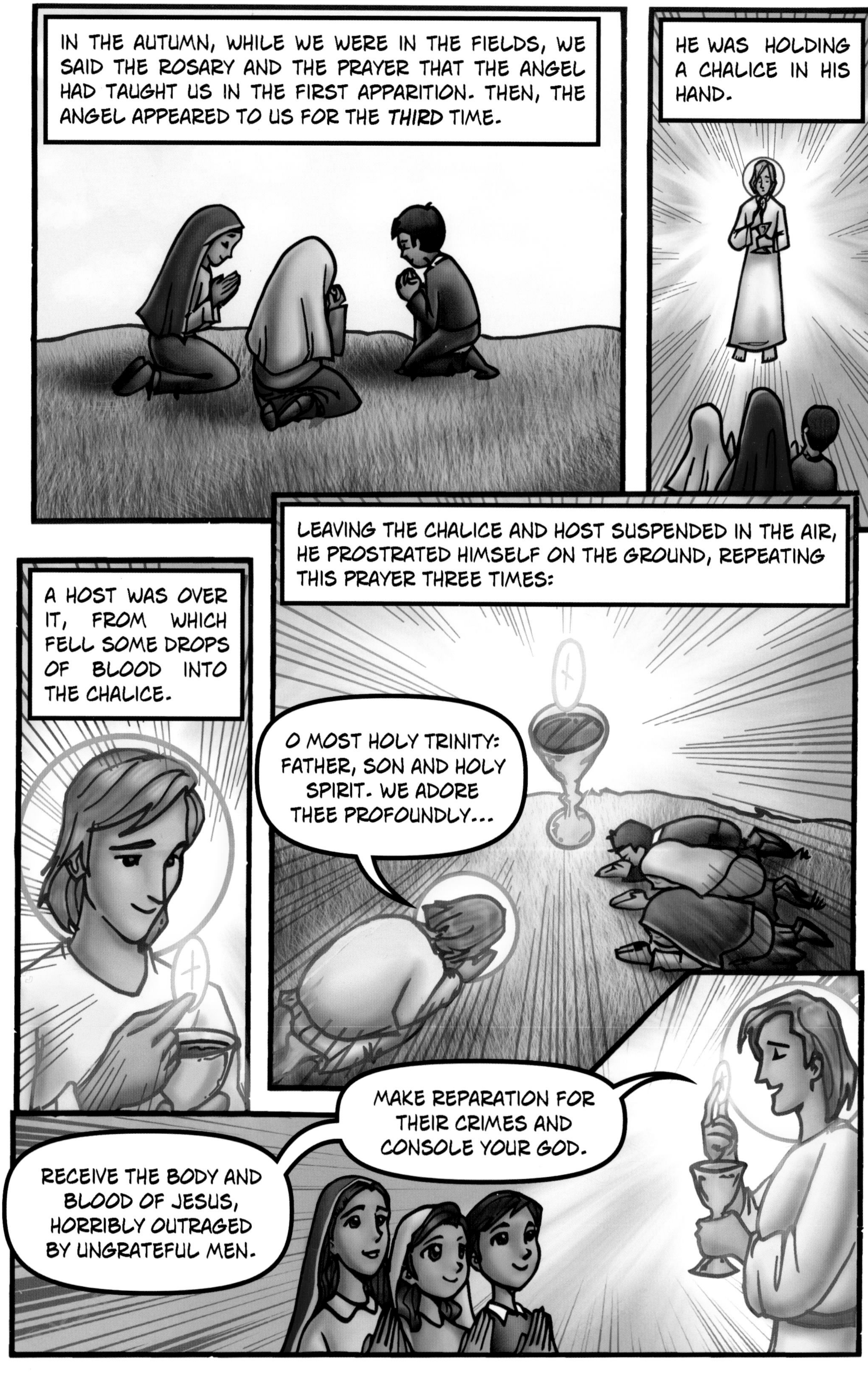
IN THE AUTUMN, WHILE WE WERE IN THE FIELDS, WE SAID THE ROSARY AND THE PRAYER THAT THE ANGEL HAD TAUGHT US IN THE FIRST APPARITION. THEN, THE ANGEL APPEARED TO US FOR THE THIRD TIME.
HE WAS HOLDING A CHALICE IN HIS HAND.
A HOST WAS OVER IT, FROM WHICH FELL SOME DROPS OF BLOOD INTO THE CHALICE.
LEAVING THE CHALICE AND HOST SUSPENDED IN THE AIR, HE PROSTRATED HIMSELF ON THE GROUND, REPEATING THIS PRAYER THREE TIMES:
O MOST HOLY TRINITY: FATHER, SON AND HOLY SPIRIT. WE ADORE THEE PROFOUNDLY...
RECEIVE THE BODY AND BLOOD OF JESUS, HORRIBLY OUTRAGED BY UNGRATEFUL MEN.
MAKE REPARATION FOR THEIR CRIMES AND CONSOLE YOUR GOD.

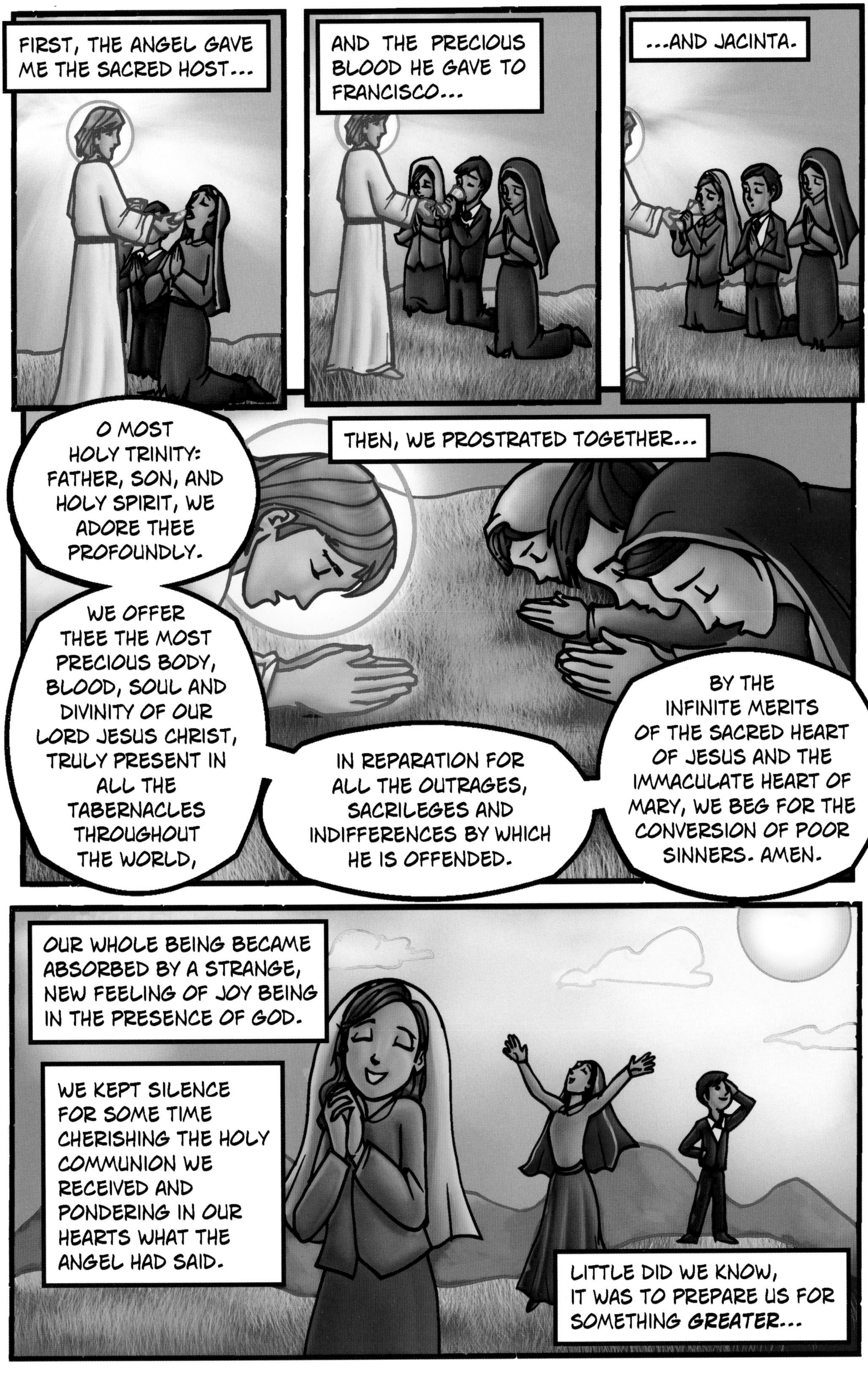
FIRST, THE ANGEL GAVE ME THE SACRED HOST...
AND THE PRECIOUS BLOOD HE GAVE TO FRANCISCO...
...AND JACINTA.
THEN, WE PROSTRATED TOGETHER...
O MOST HOLY TRINITY: FATHER, SON, AND HOLY SPIRIT, WE ADORE THEE PROFOUNDLY.
WE OFFER THEE THE MOST PRECIOUS BODY, BLOOD, SOUL AND DIVINITY OF OUR LORD JESUS CHRIST, TRULY PRESENT IN ALL THE TABERNACLES THROUGHOUT THE WORLD,
IN REPARATION FOR ALL THE OUTRAGES, SACRILEGES AND INDIFFERENCES BY WHICH HE IS OFFENDED.
BY THE INFINITE MERITS OF THE SACRED HEART OF JESUS AND THE IMMACULATE HEART OF MARY, WE BEG FOR THE CONVERSION OF POOR SINNERS. AMEN.
OUR WHOLE BEING BECAME ABSORBED BY A STRANGE, NEW FEELING OF JOY BEING IN THE PRESENCE OF GOD.
WE KEPT SILENCE FOR SOME TIME CHERISHING THE HOLY COMMUNION WE RECEIVED AND PONDERING IN OUR HEARTS WHAT THE ANGEL HAD SAID.
LITTLE DID WE KNOW, IT WAS TO PREPARE US FOR SOMETHING GREATER...

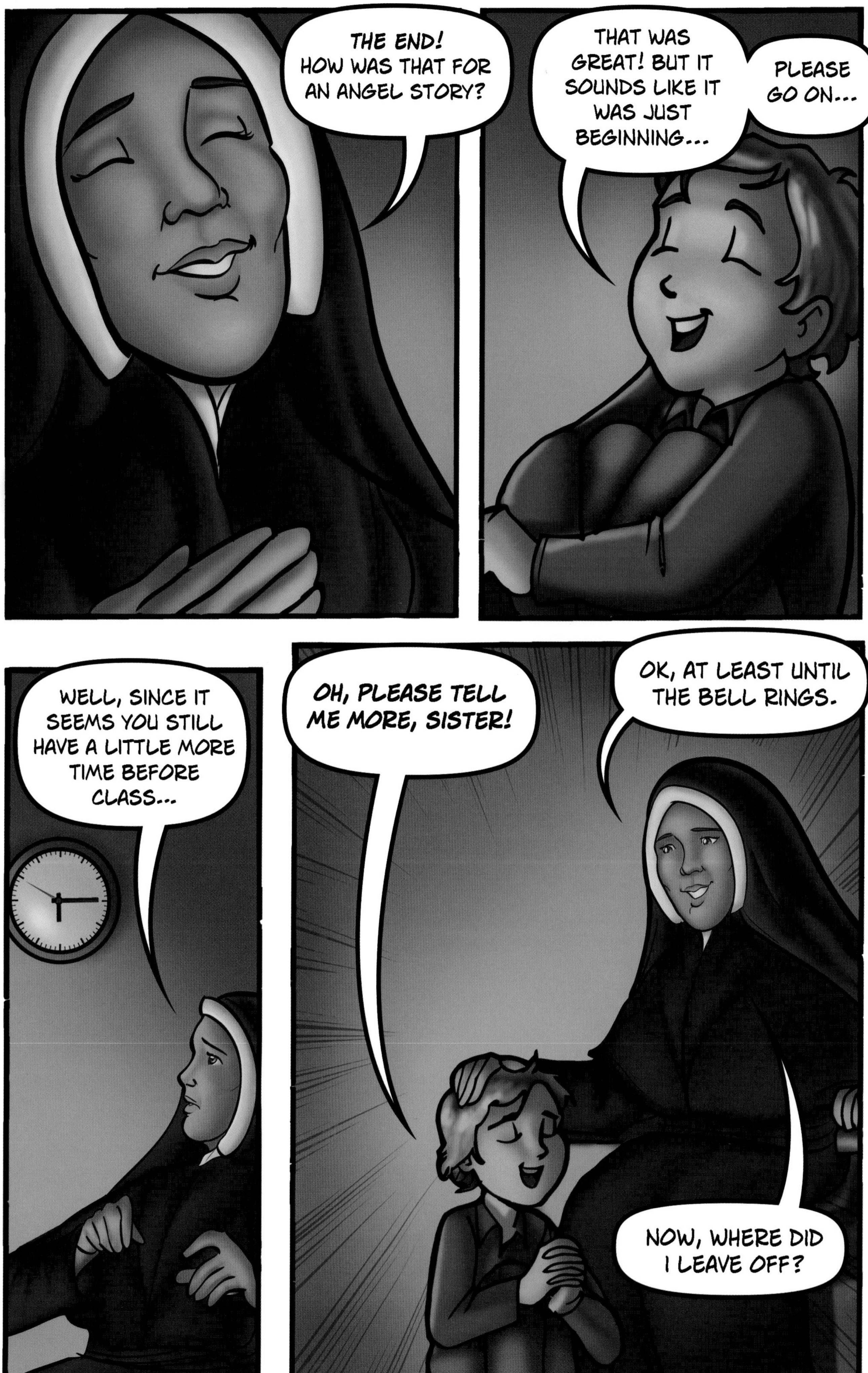
THE END! HOW WAS THAT FOR AN ANGEL STORY?
THAT WAS GREAT! BUT IT SOUNDS LIKE IT WAS JUST BEGINNING...
PLEASE GO ON...
WELL, SINCE IT SEEMS YOU STILL HAVE A LITTLE MORE TIME BEFORE CLASS...
OH, PLEASE TELL ME MORE, SISTER!
OK, AT LEAST UNTIL THE BELL RINGS.
NOW, WHERE DID I LEAVE OFF?

May 13, 1917

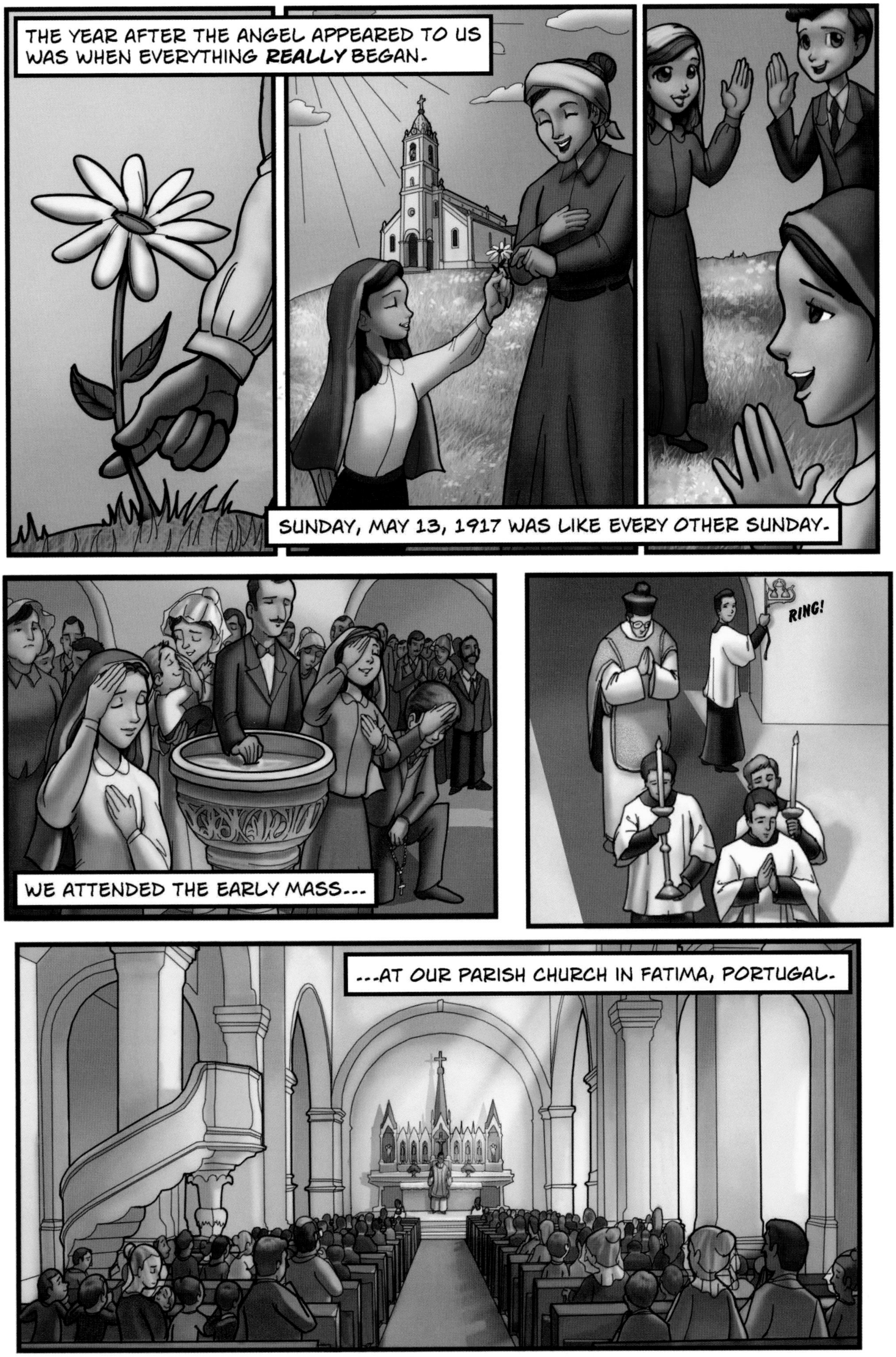
THE YEAR AFTER THE ANGEL APPEARED TO US WAS WHEN EVERYTHING REALLY BEGAN.
SUNDAY, MAY 13, 1917 WAS LIKE EVERY OTHER SUNDAY.
WE ATTENDED THE EARLY MASS...
RING!
...AT OUR PARISH CHURCH IN FATIMA, PORTUGAL.

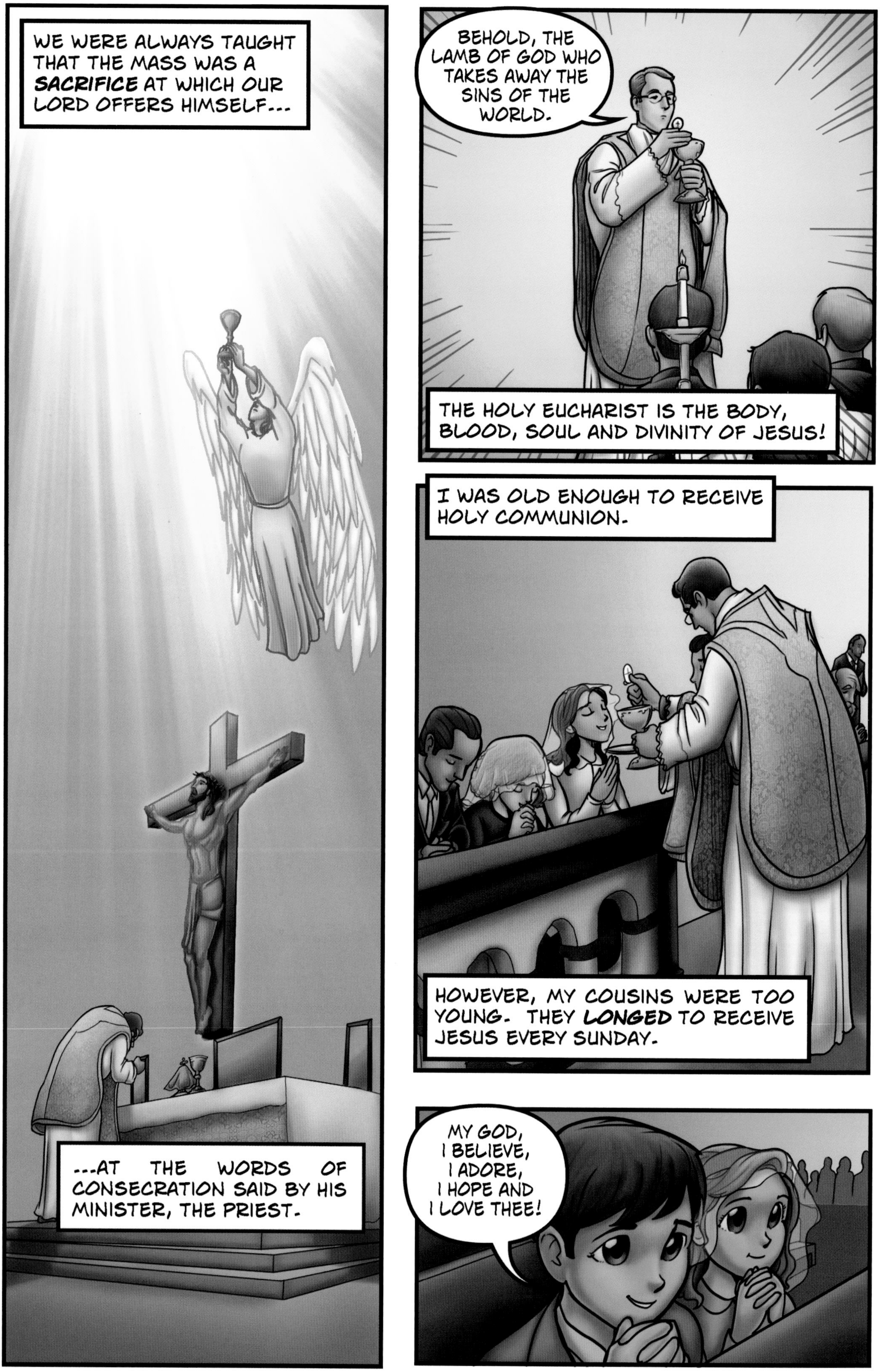
WE WERE ALWAYS TAUGHT THAT THE MASS WAS A SACRIFICE AT WHICH OUR LORD OFFERS HIMSELF...
...AT THE WORDS OF CONSECRATION SAID BY HIS MINISTER, THE PRIEST.
BEHOLD, THE LAMB OF GOD WHO TAKES AWAY THE SINS OF THE WORLD.
THE HOLY EUCHARIST IS THE BODY, BLOOD, SOUL AND DIVINITY OF JESUS!
I WAS OLD ENOUGH TO RECEIVE HOLY COMMUNION.
HOWEVER, MY COUSINS WERE TOO YOUNG. THEY LONGED TO RECEIVE JESUS EVERY SUNDAY.
MY GOD, I BELIEVE, I ADORE, I HOPE AND I LOVE THEE!

THEY WOULD EVEN EMBRACE ME AFTER MASS, KNOWING I STILL HAD JESUS *PHYSICALLY* WITHIN ME.

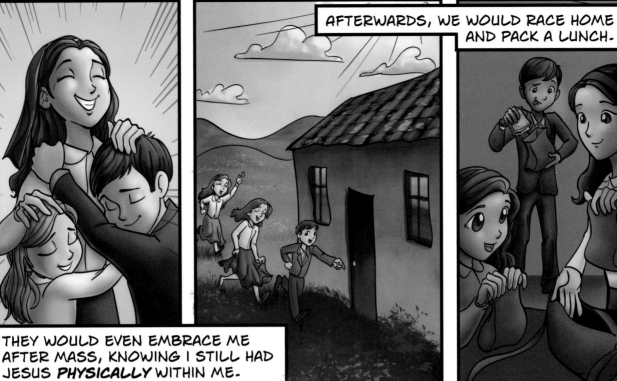

AFTERWARDS, WE WOULD RACE HOME AND PACK A LUNCH.

WE THEN TOOK THE SHEEP OUT TO PASTURE.

AT NOON, WE SAT AND HAD OUR LUNCH, FOLLOWED BY THE RECITATION OF THE ROSARY...

...OUR "SHORT VERSION."

HAIL MARY, HOLY MARY, HAIL MARY, HOLY MARY, HAIL MARY, HOLY MARY, HAIL MARY, HOLY MARY...

THEN WE COULD PLAY OUR GAMES A LOT SOONER.

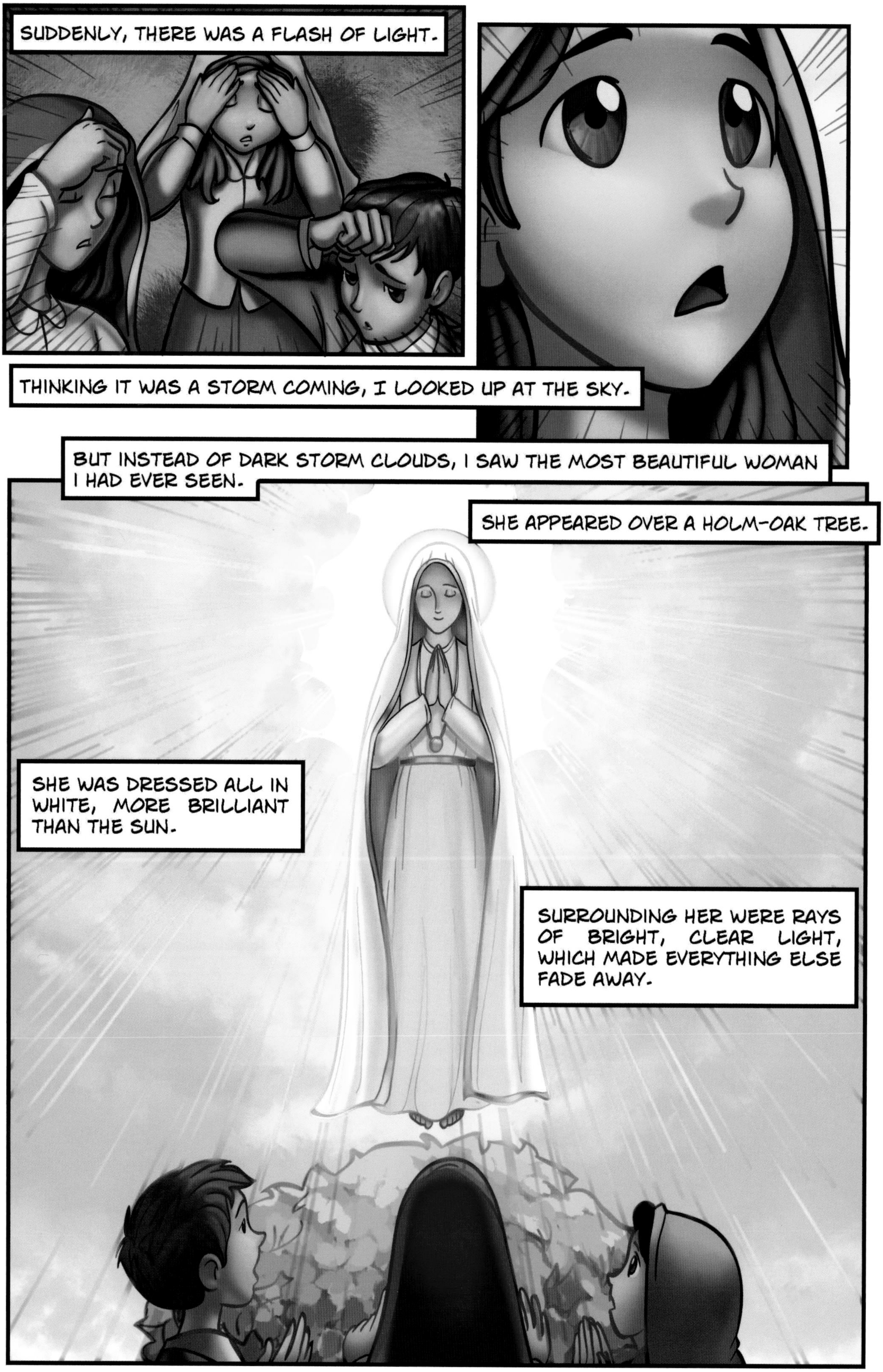
SUDDENLY, THERE WAS A FLASH OF LIGHT.
THINKING IT WAS A STORM COMING, I LOOKED UP AT THE SKY.
BUT INSTEAD OF DARK STORM CLOUDS, I SAW THE MOST BEAUTIFUL WOMAN I HAD EVER SEEN.
SHE APPEARED OVER A HOLM-OAK TREE.
SHE WAS DRESSED ALL IN WHITE, MORE BRILLIANT THAN THE SUN.
SURROUNDING HER WERE RAYS OF BRIGHT, CLEAR LIGHT, WHICH MADE EVERYTHING ELSE FADE AWAY.

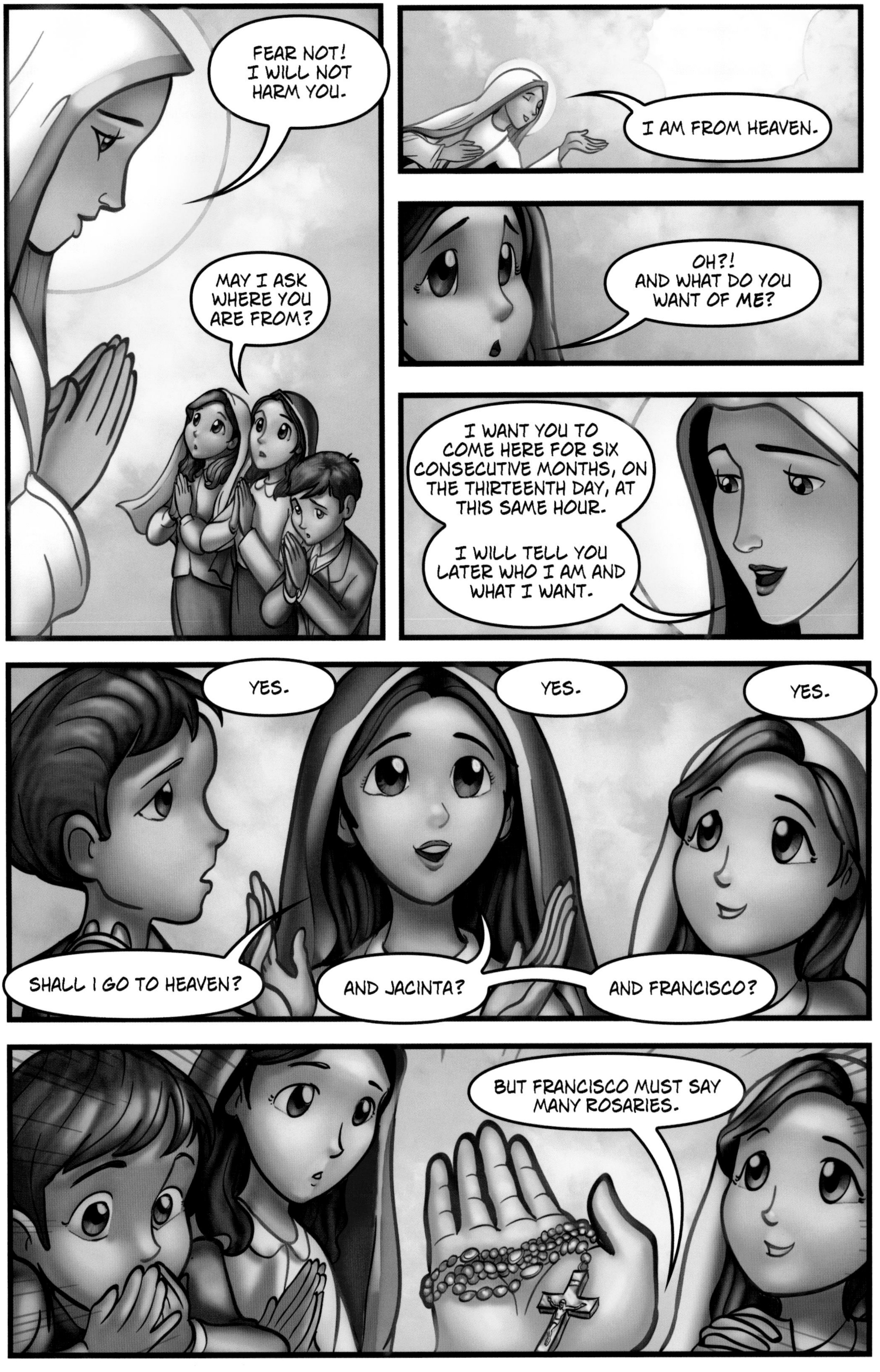
FEAR NOT! I WILL NOT HARM YOU.
MAY I ASK WHERE YOU ARE FROM?
I AM FROM HEAVEN.
OH?! AND WHAT DO YOU WANT OF ME?
I WANT YOU TO COME HERE FOR SIX CONSECUTIVE MONTHS, ON THE THIRTEENTH DAY, AT THIS SAME HOUR.
I WILL TELL YOU LATER WHO I AM AND WHAT I WANT.
SHALL I GO TO HEAVEN?
YES.
AND JACINTA?
YES.
AND FRANCISCO?
YES.
BUT FRANCISCO MUST SAY MANY ROSARIES.

AND MARIA NEVES, DAUGHTER OF JOSE NEVES, IS SHE IN HEAVEN?

YES.

AND AMELIA?

SHE IS STILL IN PURGATORY.

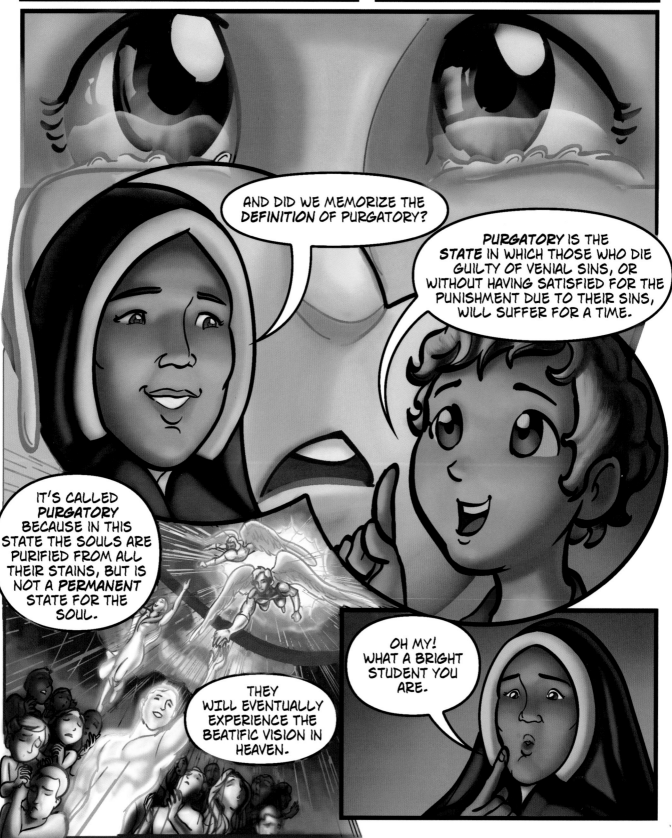

AND DID WE MEMORIZE THE DEFINITION OF PURGATORY?

PURGATORY IS THE STATE IN WHICH THOSE WHO DIE GUILTY OF VENIAL SINS, OR WITHOUT HAVING SATISFIED FOR THE PUNISHMENT DUE TO THEIR SINS, WILL SUFFER FOR A TIME.

IT'S CALLED PURGATORY BECAUSE IN THIS STATE THE SOULS ARE PURIFIED FROM ALL THEIR STAINS, BUT IS NOT A PERMANENT STATE FOR THE SOUL.

THEY WILL EVENTUALLY EXPERIENCE THE BEATIFIC VISION IN HEAVEN.

OH MY! WHAT A BRIGHT STUDENT YOU ARE.

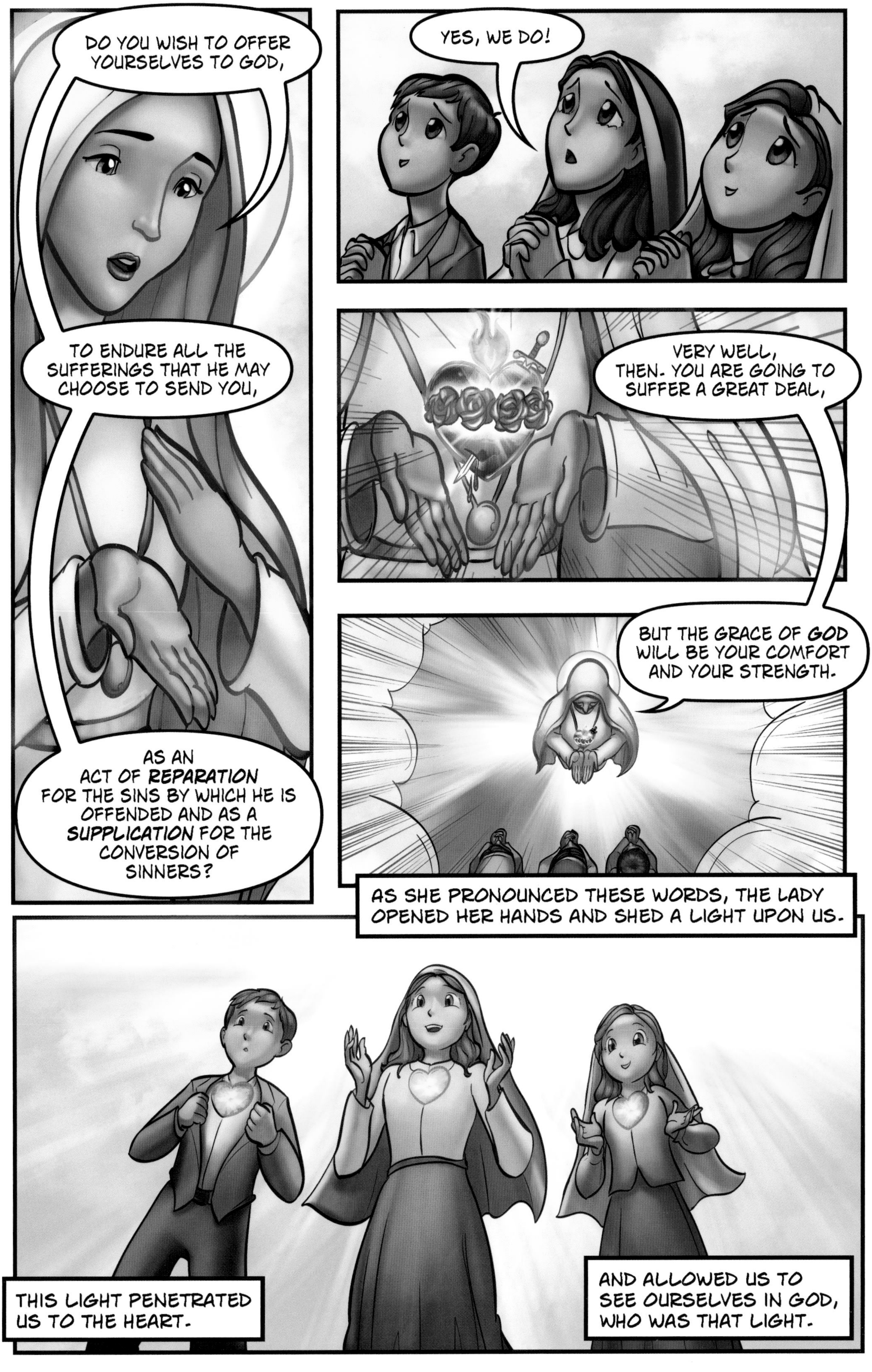
DO YOU WISH TO OFFER YOURSELVES TO GOD,
YES, WE DO!
TO ENDURE ALL THE SUFFERINGS THAT HE MAY CHOOSE TO SEND YOU,
VERY WELL, THEN. YOU ARE GOING TO SUFFER A GREAT DEAL,
BUT THE GRACE OF GOD WILL BE YOUR COMFORT AND YOUR STRENGTH.
AS AN ACT OF REPARATION FOR THE SINS BY WHICH HE IS OFFENDED AND AS A SUPPLICATION FOR THE CONVERSION OF SINNERS?
AS SHE PRONOUNCED THESE WORDS, THE LADY OPENED HER HANDS AND SHED A LIGHT UPON US.
THIS LIGHT PENETRATED US TO THE HEART.
AND ALLOWED US TO SEE OURSELVES IN GOD, WHO WAS THAT LIGHT.

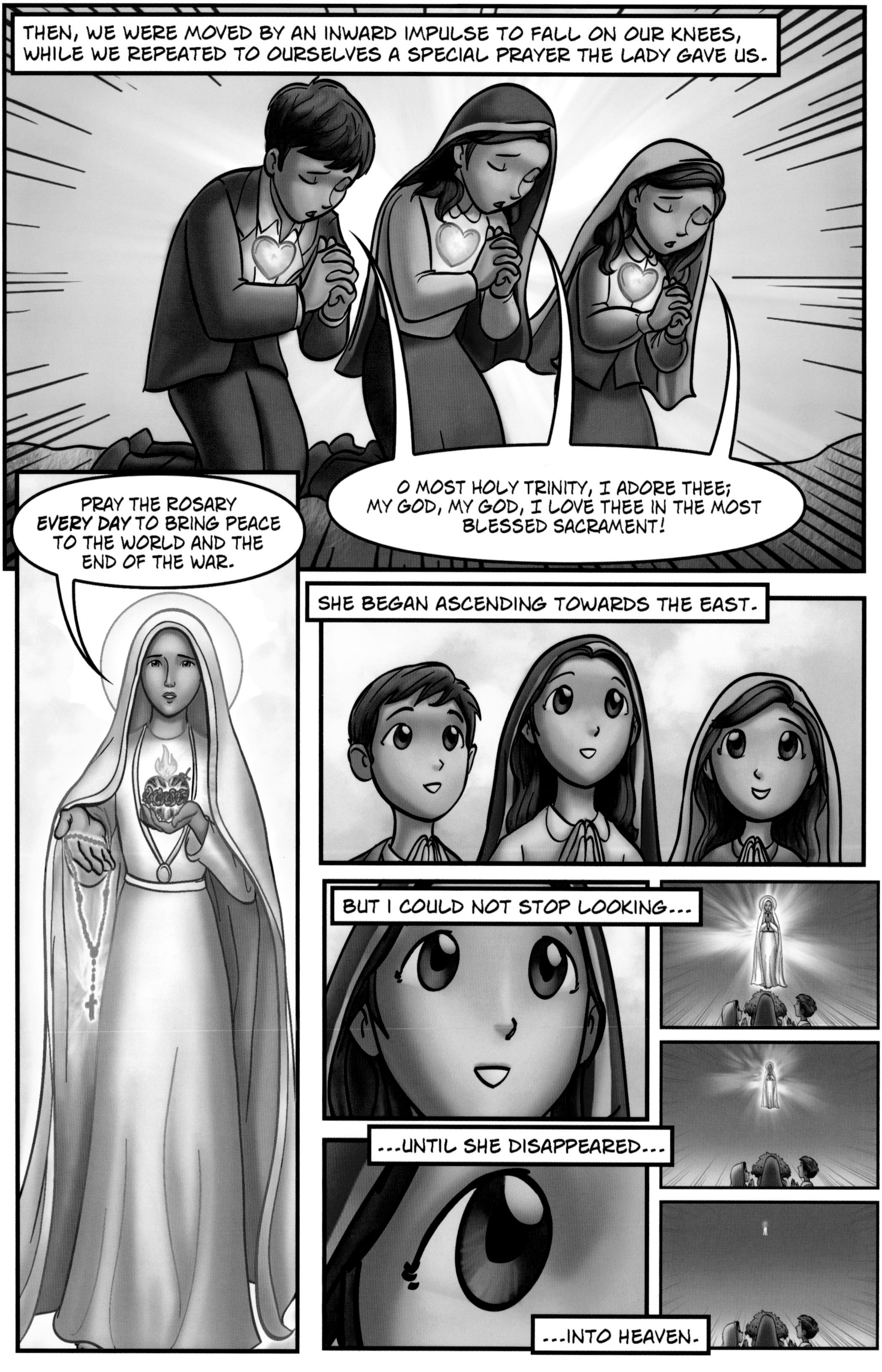
THEN, WE WERE MOVED BY AN INWARD IMPULSE TO FALL ON OUR KNEES, WHILE WE REPEATED TO OURSELVES A SPECIAL PRAYER THE LADY GAVE US.
O MOST HOLY TRINITY, I ADORE THEE; MY GOD, MY GOD, I LOVE THEE IN THE MOST BLESSED SACRAMENT!
PRAY THE ROSARY EVERY DAY TO BRING PEACE TO THE WORLD AND THE END OF THE WAR.
SHE BEGAN ASCENDING TOWARDS THE EAST.
BUT I COULD NOT STOP LOOKING...
...UNTIL SHE DISAPPEARED...
...INTO HEAVEN.

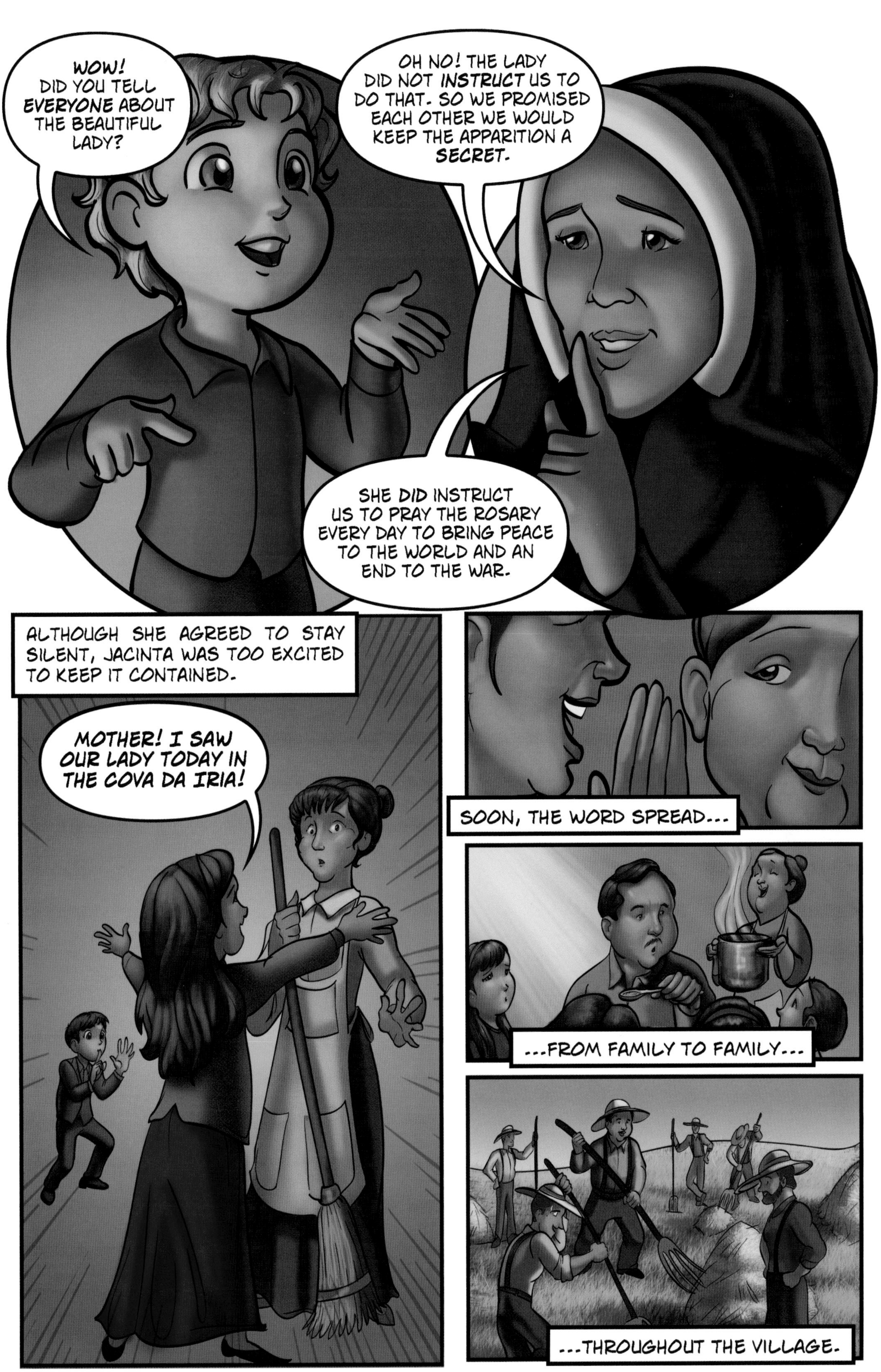

WOW! DID YOU TELL EVERYONE ABOUT THE BEAUTIFUL LADY?
OH NO! THE LADY DID NOT INSTRUCT US TO DO THAT. SO WE PROMISED EACH OTHER WE WOULD KEEP THE APPARITION A SECRET.
SHE DID INSTRUCT US TO PRAY THE ROSARY EVERY DAY TO BRING PEACE TO THE WORLD AND AN END TO THE WAR.
ALTHOUGH SHE AGREED TO STAY SILENT, JACINTA WAS TOO EXCITED TO KEEP IT CONTAINED.
MOTHER! I SAW OUR LADY TODAY IN THE COVA DA IRIA!
SOON, THE WORD SPREAD...
...FROM FAMILY TO FAMILY...
...THROUGHOUT THE VILLAGE.

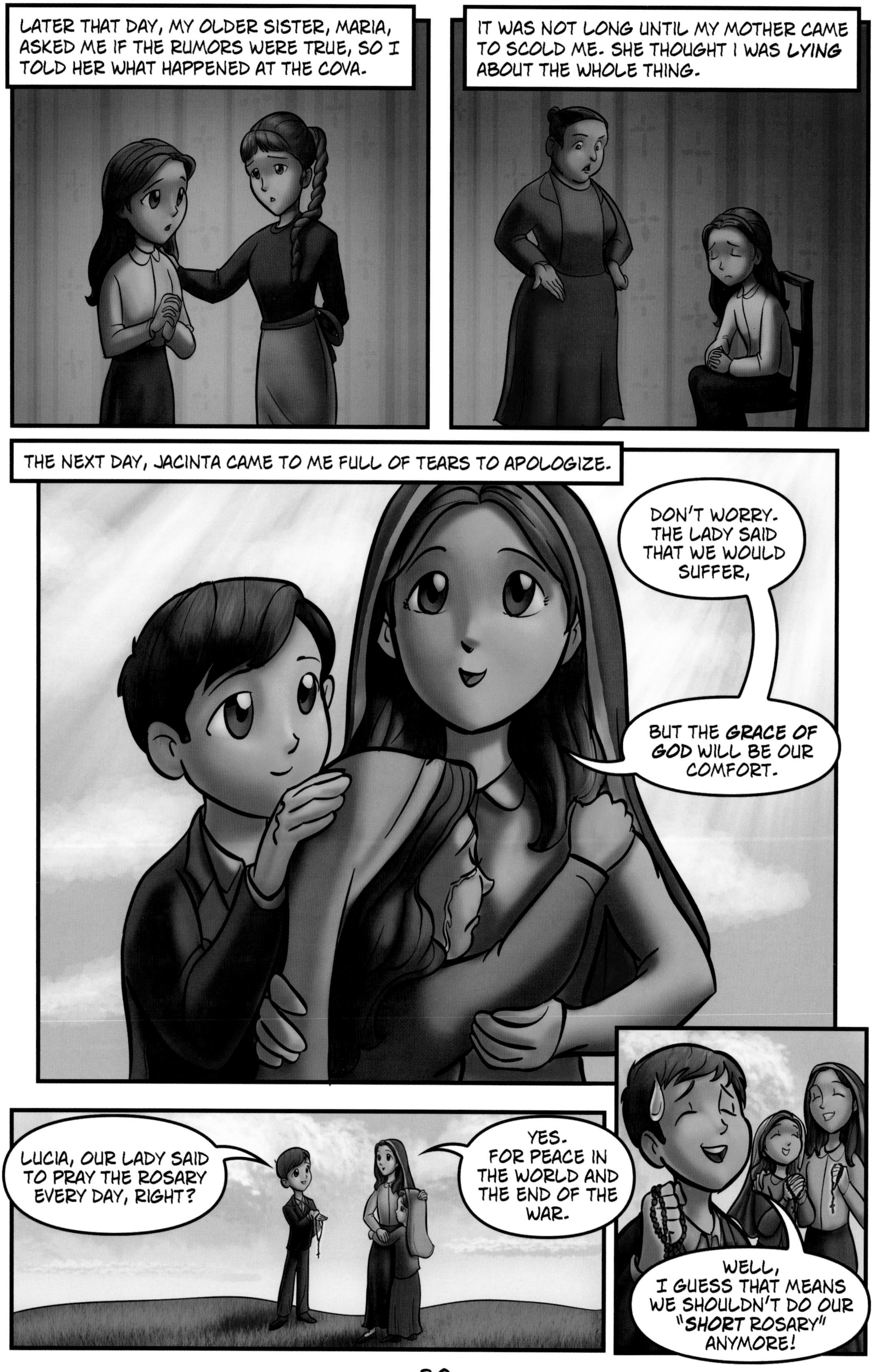
LATER THAT DAY, MY OLDER SISTER, MARIA, ASKED ME IF THE RUMORS WERE TRUE, SO I TOLD HER WHAT HAPPENED AT THE COVA.
IT WAS NOT LONG UNTIL MY MOTHER CAME TO SCOLD ME. SHE THOUGHT I WAS **LYING** ABOUT THE WHOLE THING.
THE NEXT DAY, JACINTA CAME TO ME FULL OF TEARS TO APOLOGIZE.
DON'T WORRY. THE LADY SAID THAT WE WOULD SUFFER,
BUT THE **GRACE OF GOD** WILL BE OUR COMFORT.
LUCIA, OUR LADY SAID TO PRAY THE ROSARY EVERY DAY, RIGHT?
YES. FOR PEACE IN THE WORLD AND THE END OF THE WAR.
WELL, I GUESS THAT MEANS WE SHOULDN'T DO OUR "**SHORT** ROSARY" ANYMORE!

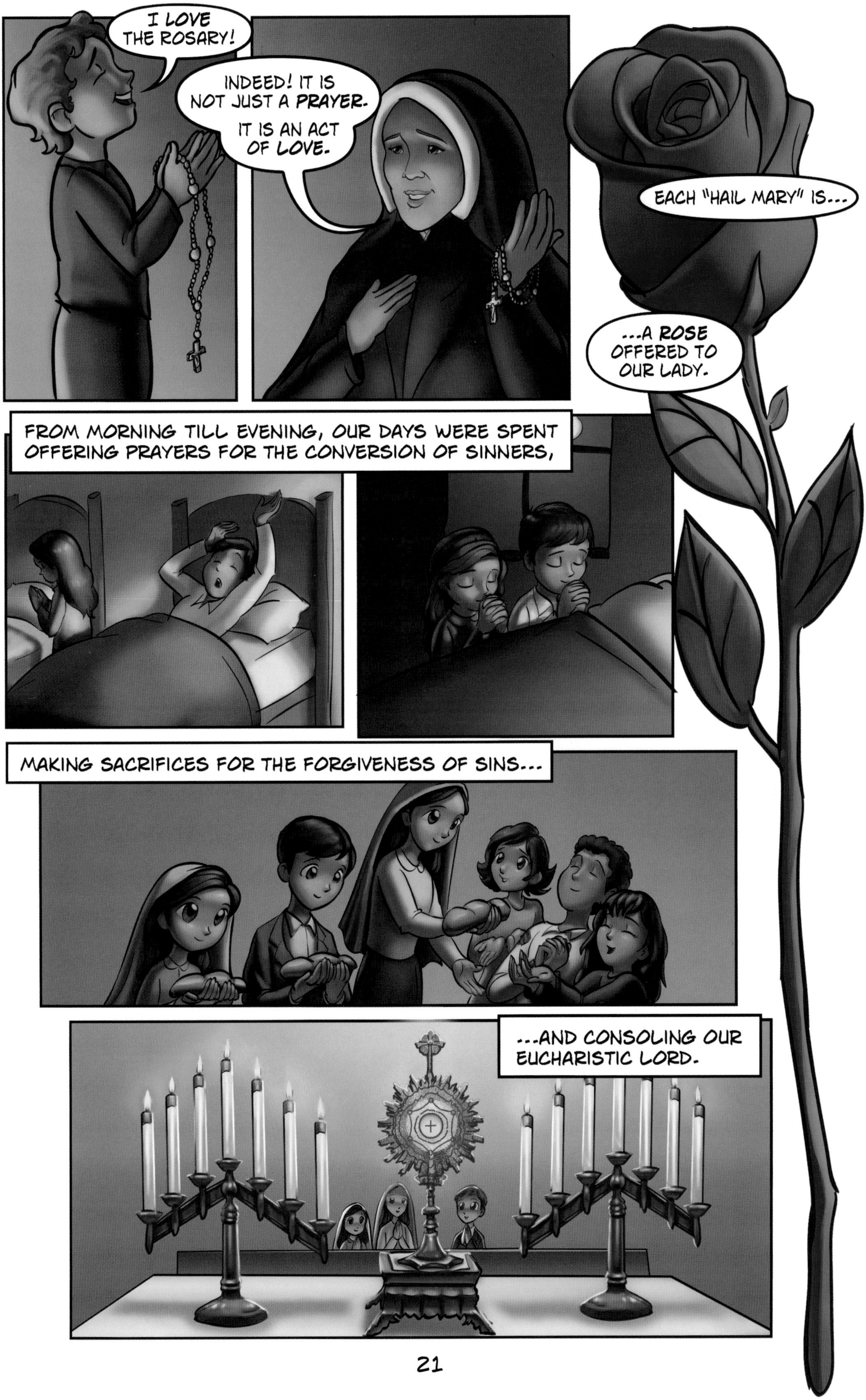
I LOVE THE ROSARY!
INDEED! IT IS NOT JUST A PRAYER.
IT IS AN ACT OF LOVE.
EACH "HAIL MARY" IS...
...A ROSE OFFERED TO OUR LADY.
FROM MORNING TILL EVENING, OUR DAYS WERE SPENT OFFERING PRAYERS FOR THE CONVERSION OF SINNERS,
MAKING SACRIFICES FOR THE FORGIVENESS OF SINS...
...AND CONSOLING OUR EUCHARISTIC LORD.

BEFORE WE KNEW IT, THE THIRTEENTH OF **JUNE** HAD QUICKLY ARRIVED.

AFTER WE TOOK THE SHEEP IN THE MORNING, WE WENT HOME TO CHANGE AND PUT ON OUR BEST BEFORE OUR APPOINTED TIME WITH "THE LADY."

SINCE WORD HAD SPREAD SO FAR AND WIDE, MANY ALSO CAME FROM NEIGHBORING VILLAGES TO JOIN US.

TOGETHER, WE PRAYED A ROSARY WHILE WE WAITED FOR OUR HEAVENLY VISITOR.

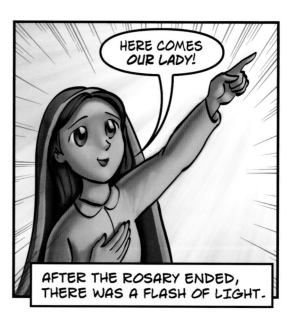

HERE COMES OUR LADY!

AFTER THE ROSARY ENDED, THERE WAS A FLASH OF LIGHT.

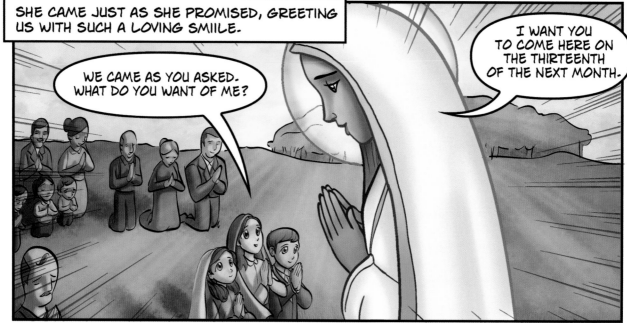

SHE CAME JUST AS SHE PROMISED, GREETING US WITH SUCH A LOVING SMIILE.

WE CAME AS YOU ASKED. WHAT DO YOU WANT OF ME?

I WANT YOU TO COME HERE ON THE THIRTEENTH OF THE NEXT MONTH.

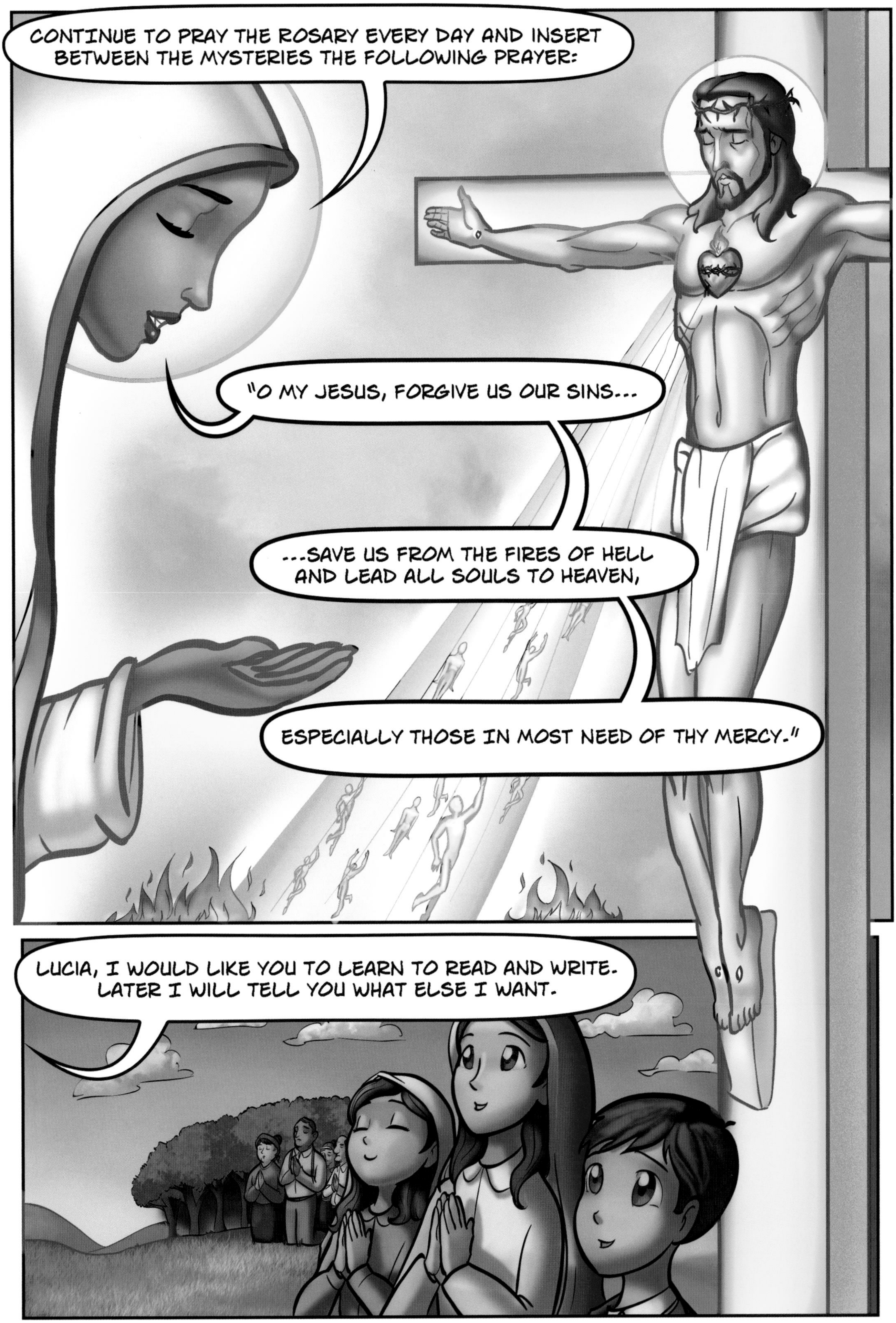
CONTINUE TO PRAY THE ROSARY EVERY DAY AND INSERT BETWEEN THE MYSTERIES THE FOLLOWING PRAYER:
"O MY JESUS, FORGIVE US OUR SINS...
...SAVE US FROM THE FIRES OF HELL AND LEAD ALL SOULS TO HEAVEN,
ESPECIALLY THOSE IN MOST NEED OF THY MERCY."
LUCIA, I WOULD LIKE YOU TO LEARN TO READ AND WRITE. LATER I WILL TELL YOU WHAT ELSE I WANT.

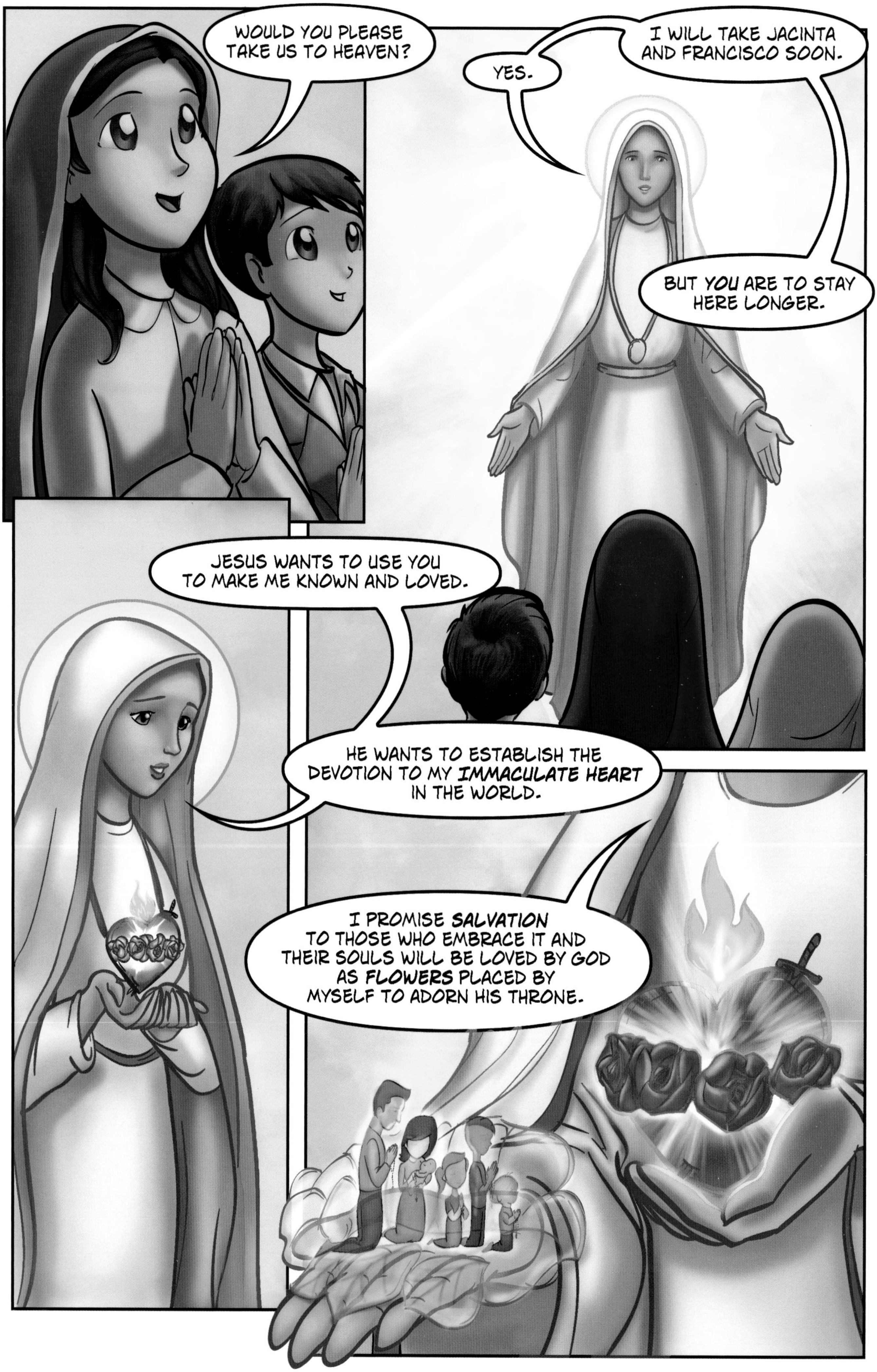
WOULD YOU PLEASE TAKE US TO HEAVEN?
YES.
I WILL TAKE JACINTA AND FRANCISCO SOON.
BUT *YOU* ARE TO STAY HERE LONGER.
JESUS WANTS TO USE YOU TO MAKE ME KNOWN AND LOVED.
HE WANTS TO ESTABLISH THE DEVOTION TO MY **IMMACULATE HEART** IN THE WORLD.
I PROMISE **SALVATION** TO THOSE WHO EMBRACE IT AND THEIR SOULS WILL BE LOVED BY GOD AS **FLOWERS** PLACED BY MYSELF TO ADORN HIS THRONE.

AM I GOING TO STAY HERE ALONE?

NO, MY DAUGHTER. I WILL *NEVER* LEAVE YOU.

MY *IMMACULATE HEART* WILL BE YOUR *REFUGE* AND THE *WAY* THAT WILL LEAD YOU TO GOD.

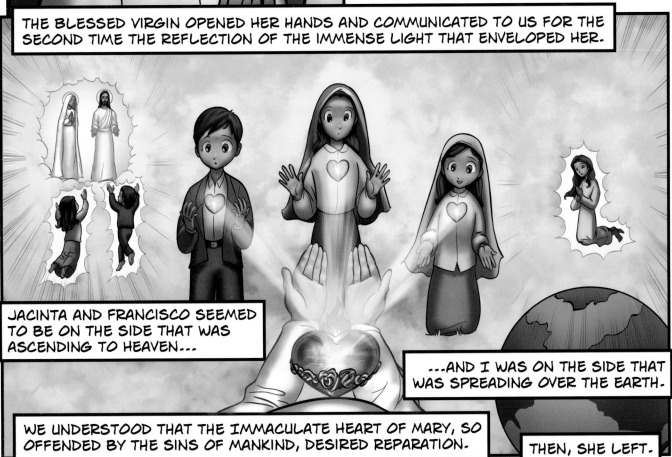

THE BLESSED VIRGIN OPENED HER HANDS AND COMMUNICATED TO US FOR THE SECOND TIME THE REFLECTION OF THE IMMENSE LIGHT THAT ENVELOPED HER.

JACINTA AND FRANCISCO SEEMED TO BE ON THE SIDE THAT WAS ASCENDING TO HEAVEN...

...AND I WAS ON THE SIDE THAT WAS SPREADING OVER THE EARTH.

WE UNDERSTOOD THAT THE IMMACULATE HEART OF MARY, SO OFFENDED BY THE SINS OF MANKIND, DESIRED REPARATION.

THEN, SHE LEFT.

25

YOU MUST BE SO HAPPY THAT OUR LADY PROMISED YOU HEAVEN. IT'S SO WONDERFUL!

OH YES, I DREAM OF HEAVEN EVERYDAY. BUT THE TRUTH IS THAT GOD WANTS US **ALL** TO EXPERIENCE HEAVEN.

HEAVEN IS THE STATE OF EVERLASTING LIFE IN WHICH WE SEE GOD FACE-TO-FACE, ARE MADE LIKE HIM IN GLORY, AND ENJOY ETERNAL HAPPINESS.

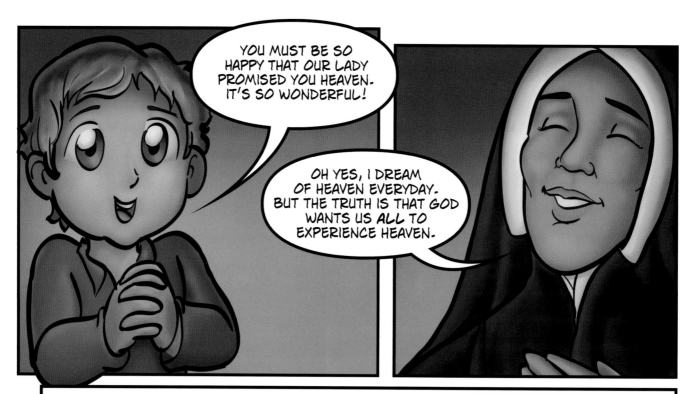

IN THE GOSPEL ACCORDING TO ST. MATTHEW, JESUS TEACHES THE BEATITUDES. ONE OF WHICH IS "BLESSED ARE THE PURE OF HEART, FOR THEY SHALL SEE GOD."

THAT'S WHY IT IS IMPORTANT TO REMAIN PURE AND AVOID SIN IN ORDER TO BE **WORTHY** OF HEAVEN.

THAT'S TRUE, SISTER! AND WHAT DID OUR LADY SAY ON HER NEXT VISIT?

WELL, ON THE 13TH OF JULY, OUR LADY APPEARED AS BEFORE, BUT THIS TIME...

...SHE DID NOT GREET US WITH HER USUAL SMILE.

26

July 13, 1917

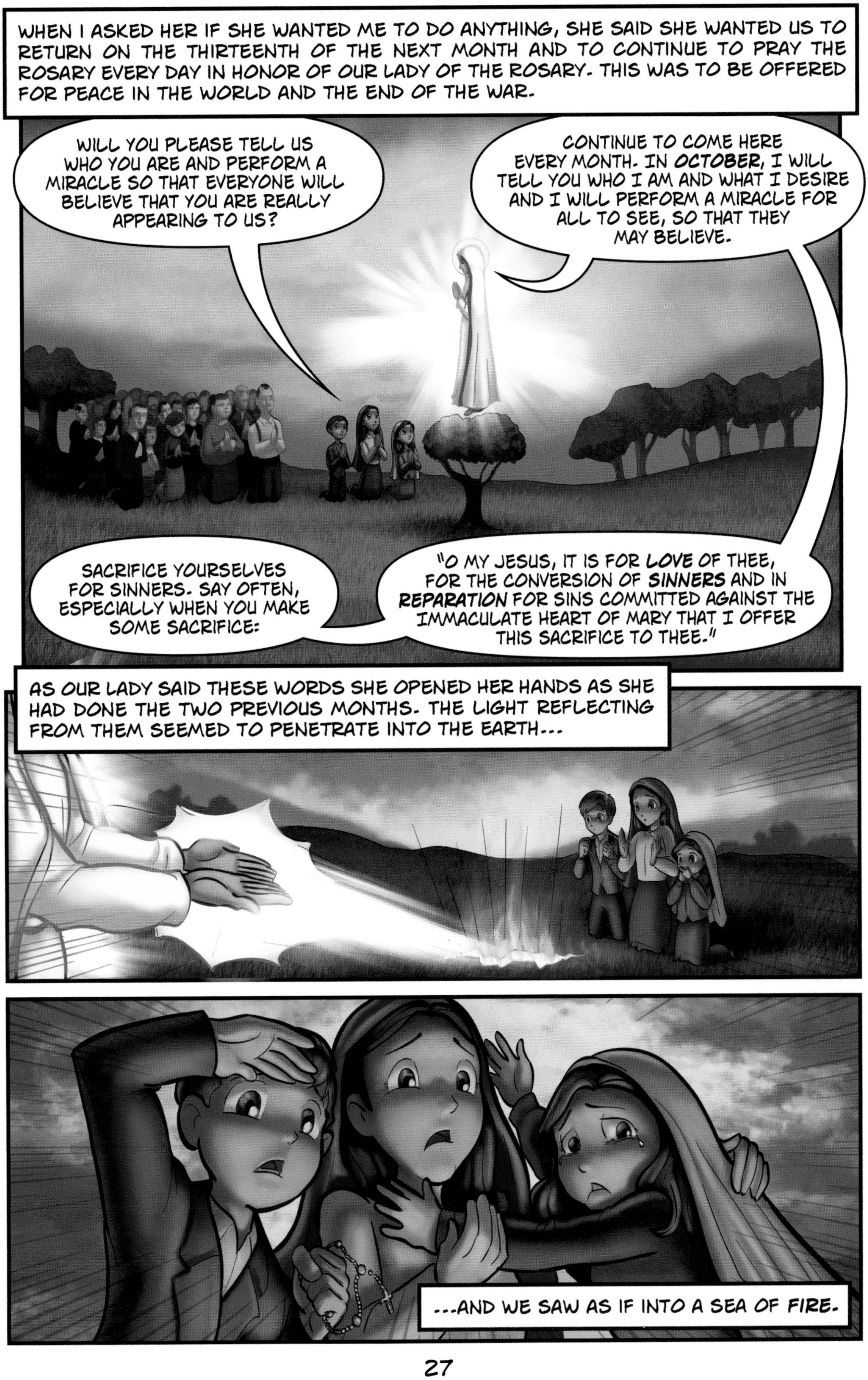
WHEN I ASKED HER IF SHE WANTED ME TO DO ANYTHING, SHE SAID SHE WANTED US TO RETURN ON THE THIRTEENTH OF THE NEXT MONTH AND TO CONTINUE TO PRAY THE ROSARY EVERY DAY IN HONOR OF OUR LADY OF THE ROSARY. THIS WAS TO BE OFFERED FOR PEACE IN THE WORLD AND THE END OF THE WAR.
WILL YOU PLEASE TELL US WHO YOU ARE AND PERFORM A MIRACLE SO THAT EVERYONE WILL BELIEVE THAT YOU ARE REALLY APPEARING TO US?
CONTINUE TO COME HERE EVERY MONTH. IN **OCTOBER**, I WILL TELL YOU WHO I AM AND WHAT I DESIRE AND I WILL PERFORM A MIRACLE FOR ALL TO SEE, SO THAT THEY MAY BELIEVE.
SACRIFICE YOURSELVES FOR SINNERS. SAY OFTEN, ESPECIALLY WHEN YOU MAKE SOME SACRIFICE:
"O MY JESUS, IT IS FOR **LOVE** OF THEE, FOR THE CONVERSION OF **SINNERS** AND IN ***REPARATION*** FOR SINS COMMITTED AGAINST THE IMMACULATE HEART OF MARY THAT I OFFER THIS SACRIFICE TO THEE."
AS OUR LADY SAID THESE WORDS SHE OPENED HER HANDS AS SHE HAD DONE THE TWO PREVIOUS MONTHS. THE LIGHT REFLECTING FROM THEM SEEMED TO PENETRATE INTO THE EARTH...
...AND WE SAW AS IF INTO A SEA OF ***FIRE***.

IMMERSED IN THAT FIRE WERE DEVILS AND **SOULS** IN HUMAN FORM. THE SIGHT BECAME EVEN MORE HORRIFIC WITH THE SOUND OF WAILING AND CRIES OF PAIN AND DESPAIR.

AHHHH!!!

AHHHH!!!

AHHHH!!!

OH, OUR LADY!

CRRRR...

RSSSH...

SHOOM!

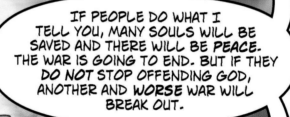

YOU HAVE SEEN HELL WHERE THE SOULS OF POOR SINNERS GO. TO SAVE THEM, **GOD** WANTS TO ESTABLISH THROUGHOUT THE WORLD THE DEVOTION TO MY IMMACULATE HEART.

IF PEOPLE DO WHAT I TELL YOU, MANY SOULS WILL BE SAVED AND THERE WILL BE **PEACE**. THE WAR IS GOING TO END. BUT IF THEY **DO NOT** STOP OFFENDING GOD, ANOTHER AND **WORSE** WAR WILL BREAK OUT.

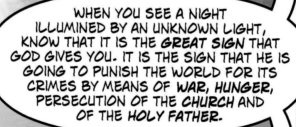

WHEN YOU SEE A NIGHT ILLUMINED BY AN UNKNOWN LIGHT, KNOW THAT IT IS THE **GREAT SIGN** THAT GOD GIVES YOU. IT IS THE SIGN THAT HE IS GOING TO PUNISH THE WORLD FOR ITS CRIMES BY MEANS OF **WAR, HUNGER**, PERSECUTION OF THE **CHURCH** AND OF THE **HOLY FATHER**.

TO **PREVENT** THIS, I SHALL COME TO ASK FOR THE CONSECRATION OF RUSSIA TO MY IMMACULATE HEART AND THE **COMMUNION OF REPARATION** ON FIVE FIRST-SATURDAYS.

28

THAT IS WHY SHE DID NOT SMILE. OUR LADY WAS SADDENED BY THE REALITY THAT MANY SOULS GO TO HELL.
SADLY, TOO MANY ACCEPT THE EXISTENCE OF HEAVEN WITHOUT AVOIDING THE SINS THAT LEAD THEM TO HELL.
OUR LADY ALSO REVEALED THAT, "MORE SOULS GO TO HELL BECAUSE OF SINS OF THE FLESH THAN FOR ANY OTHER REASON."
"FASHIONS WILL BE INTRODUCED THAT WILL OFFEND OUR LORD VERY MUCH."

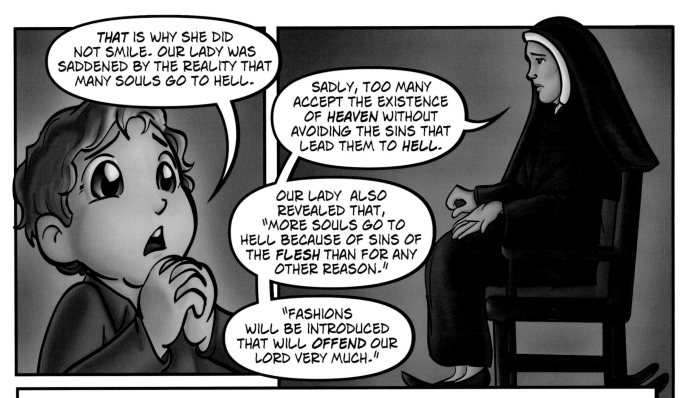

THE SINS OF THE WORLD ARE VERY GREAT. IF MEN ONLY KNEW WHAT ETERNITY IS, THEY WOULD DO EVERYTHING IN THEIR POWER TO CHANGE THEIR LIVES. WE *MUST* AVOID...

THE 7 DEADLY SINS (CCC #1866, BALTIMORE CATECHISM #3)

PRIDE — *PRIDE* IS AN EXCESSIVE LOVE OF OUR OWN ABILITY; IT LEADS US TO RATHER SINFULLY DISOBEY THAN HUMBLE OURSELVES.

ANGER — *ANGER* IS AN EXCESSIVE EMOTION OF THE MIND EXCITED AGAINST ANY PERSON OR THING, OR IT IS AN EXCESSIVE DESIRE FOR REVENGE.

ENVY — *ENVY* IS A FEELING OF SORROW AT ANOTHER'S GOOD FORTUNE AND JOY AT THE EVIL THAT COMES TO HIM.

GREED — *GREED* IS AN EXCESSIVE DESIRE FOR WORLDLY THINGS. IT LEADS US TO UNKINDNESS, DISHONESTY, DECEIT AND LACK OF CHARITY.

GLUTTONY — *GLUTTONY* IS AN EXCESSIVE DESIRE FOR FOOD OR DRINK.

SLOTH — *SLOTH* IS A LAZINESS OF THE MIND AND BODY, THROUGH WHICH WE NEGLECT OUR DUTIES ON ACCOUNT OF THE LABOR THEY REQUIRE.

LUST — *LUST* IS AN EXCESSIVE DESIRE FOR THE SINFUL PLEASURES FORBIDDEN BY THE SIXTH COMMANDMENT.

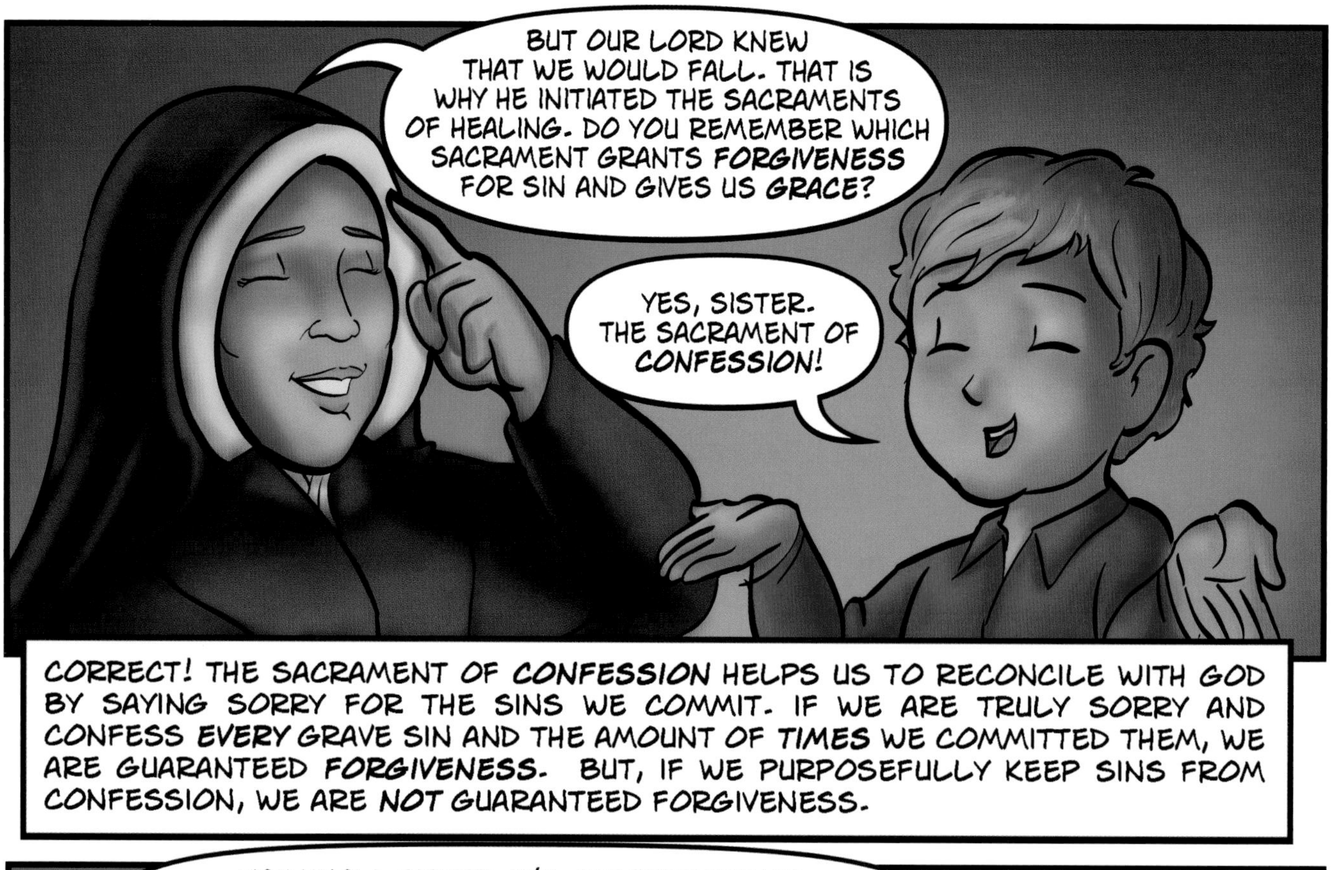
BUT OUR LORD KNEW THAT WE WOULD FALL. THAT IS WHY HE INITIATED THE SACRAMENTS OF HEALING. DO YOU REMEMBER WHICH SACRAMENT GRANTS ***FORGIVENESS*** FOR SIN AND GIVES US ***GRACE***?
YES, SISTER. THE SACRAMENT OF ***CONFESSION***!

CORRECT! THE SACRAMENT OF ***CONFESSION*** HELPS US TO RECONCILE WITH GOD BY SAYING SORRY FOR THE SINS WE COMMIT. IF WE ARE TRULY SORRY AND CONFESS ***EVERY*** GRAVE SIN AND THE AMOUNT OF ***TIMES*** WE COMMITTED THEM, WE ARE GUARANTEED ***FORGIVENESS***. BUT, IF WE PURPOSEFULLY KEEP SINS FROM CONFESSION, WE ARE ***NOT*** GUARANTEED FORGIVENESS.

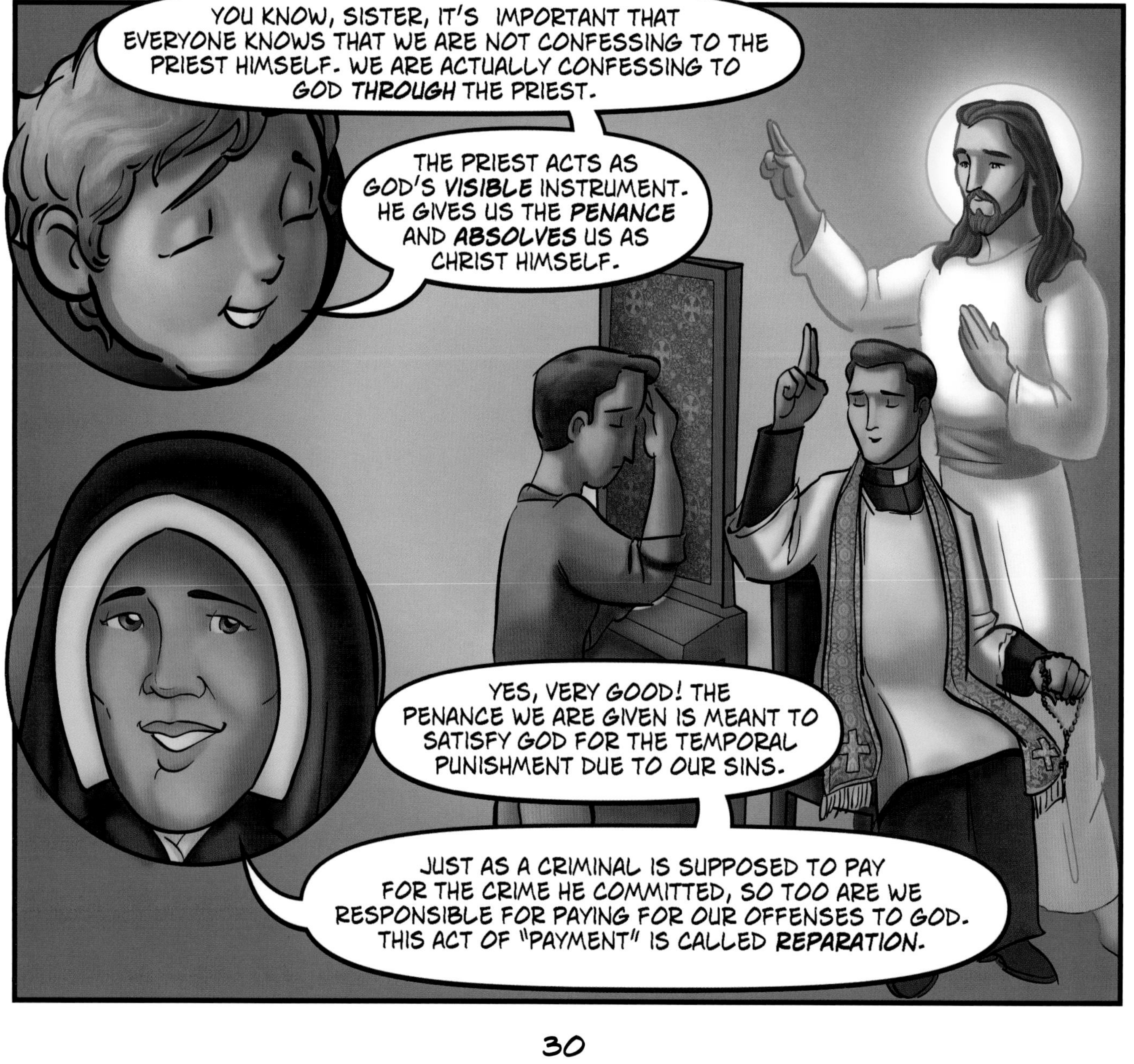
YOU KNOW, SISTER, IT'S IMPORTANT THAT EVERYONE KNOWS THAT WE ARE NOT CONFESSING TO THE PRIEST HIMSELF. WE ARE ACTUALLY CONFESSING TO GOD ***THROUGH*** THE PRIEST.
THE PRIEST ACTS AS GOD'S ***VISIBLE*** INSTRUMENT. HE GIVES US THE ***PENANCE*** AND ***ABSOLVES*** US AS CHRIST HIMSELF.
YES, VERY ***GOOD***! THE PENANCE WE ARE GIVEN IS MEANT TO SATISFY GOD FOR THE TEMPORAL PUNISHMENT DUE TO OUR SINS.
JUST AS A CRIMINAL IS SUPPOSED TO PAY FOR THE CRIME HE COMMITTED, SO TOO ARE WE RESPONSIBLE FOR PAYING FOR OUR OFFENSES TO GOD. THIS ACT OF "PAYMENT" IS CALLED ***REPARATION***.

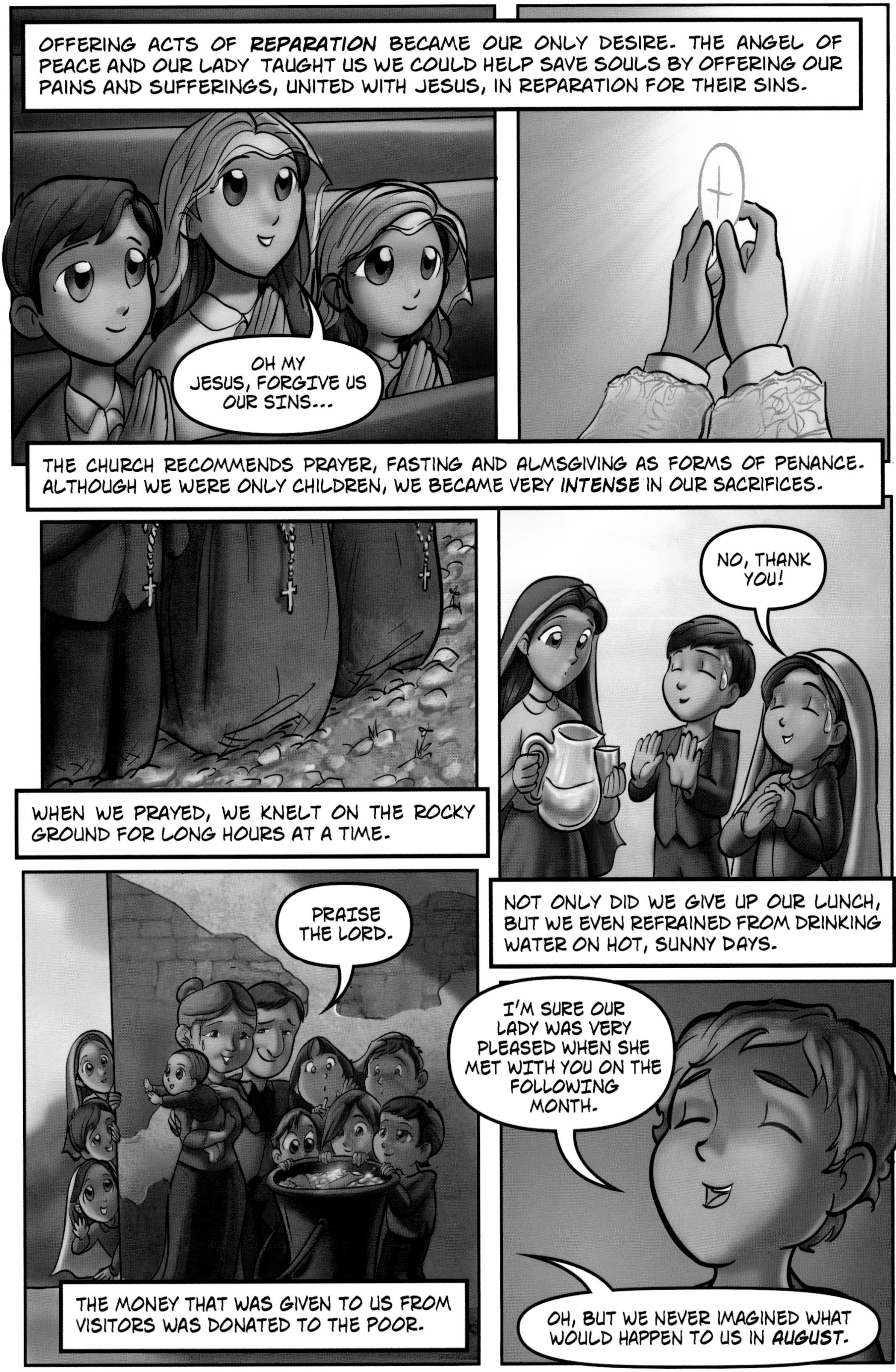
OFFERING ACTS OF REPARATION BECAME OUR ONLY DESIRE. THE ANGEL OF PEACE AND OUR LADY TAUGHT US WE COULD HELP SAVE SOULS BY OFFERING OUR PAINS AND SUFFERINGS, UNITED WITH JESUS, IN REPARATION FOR THEIR SINS.
OH MY JESUS, FORGIVE US OUR SINS...
THE CHURCH RECOMMENDS PRAYER, FASTING AND ALMSGIVING AS FORMS OF PENANCE. ALTHOUGH WE WERE ONLY CHILDREN, WE BECAME VERY INTENSE IN OUR SACRIFICES.
WHEN WE PRAYED, WE KNELT ON THE ROCKY GROUND FOR LONG HOURS AT A TIME.
NO, THANK YOU!
NOT ONLY DID WE GIVE UP OUR LUNCH, BUT WE EVEN REFRAINED FROM DRINKING WATER ON HOT, SUNNY DAYS.
PRAISE THE LORD.
THE MONEY THAT WAS GIVEN TO US FROM VISITORS WAS DONATED TO THE POOR.
I'M SURE OUR LADY WAS VERY PLEASED WHEN SHE MET WITH YOU ON THE FOLLOWING MONTH.
OH, BUT WE NEVER IMAGINED WHAT WOULD HAPPEN TO US IN AUGUST.

August 13, 1917

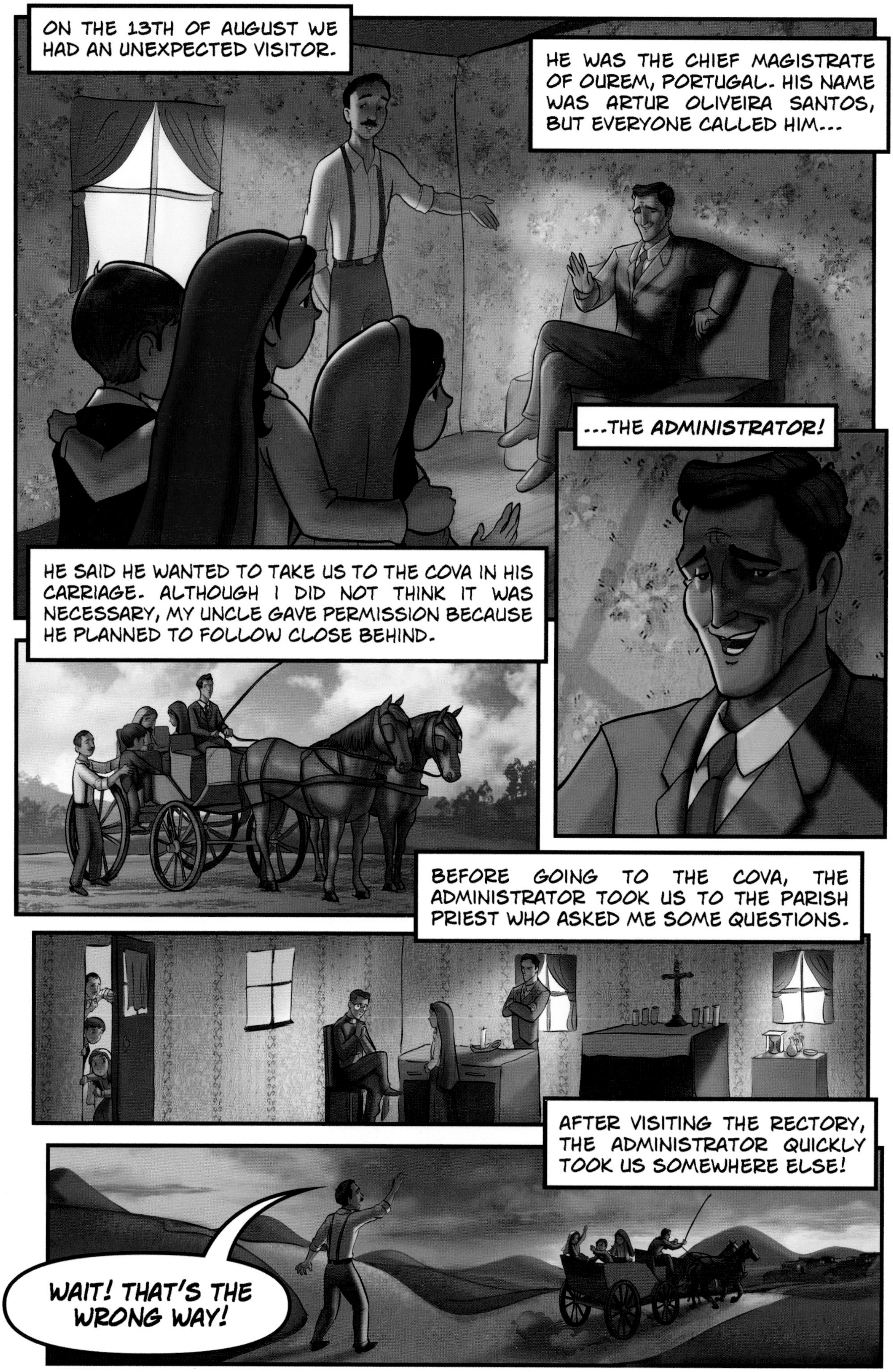

ON THE 13TH OF AUGUST WE HAD AN UNEXPECTED VISITOR.
HE WAS THE CHIEF MAGISTRATE OF OUREM, PORTUGAL. HIS NAME WAS ARTUR OLIVEIRA SANTOS, BUT EVERYONE CALLED HIM...
...THE ADMINISTRATOR!
HE SAID HE WANTED TO TAKE US TO THE COVA IN HIS CARRIAGE. ALTHOUGH I DID NOT THINK IT WAS NECESSARY, MY UNCLE GAVE PERMISSION BECAUSE HE PLANNED TO FOLLOW CLOSE BEHIND.
BEFORE GOING TO THE COVA, THE ADMINISTRATOR TOOK US TO THE PARISH PRIEST WHO ASKED ME SOME QUESTIONS.
AFTER VISITING THE RECTORY, THE ADMINISTRATOR QUICKLY TOOK US SOMEWHERE ELSE!
WAIT! THAT'S THE WRONG WAY!

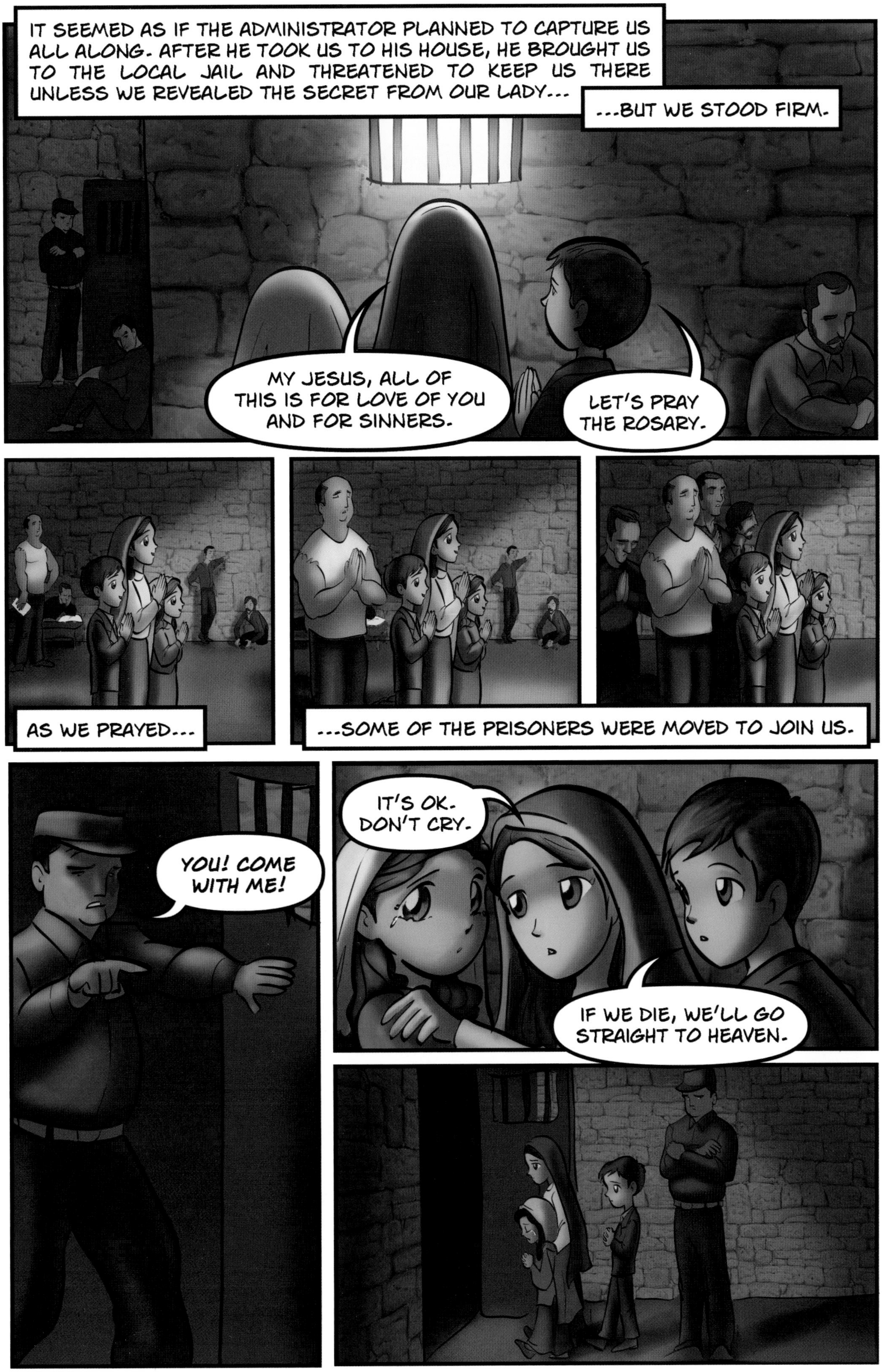
IT SEEMED AS IF THE ADMINISTRATOR PLANNED TO CAPTURE US ALL ALONG. AFTER HE TOOK US TO HIS HOUSE, HE BROUGHT US TO THE LOCAL JAIL AND THREATENED TO KEEP US THERE UNLESS WE REVEALED THE SECRET FROM OUR LADY...
...BUT WE STOOD FIRM.
MY JESUS, ALL OF THIS IS FOR LOVE OF YOU AND FOR SINNERS.
LET'S PRAY THE ROSARY.
AS WE PRAYED...
...SOME OF THE PRISONERS WERE MOVED TO JOIN US.
YOU! COME WITH ME!
IT'S OK. DON'T CRY.
IF WE DIE, WE'LL GO STRAIGHT TO HEAVEN.

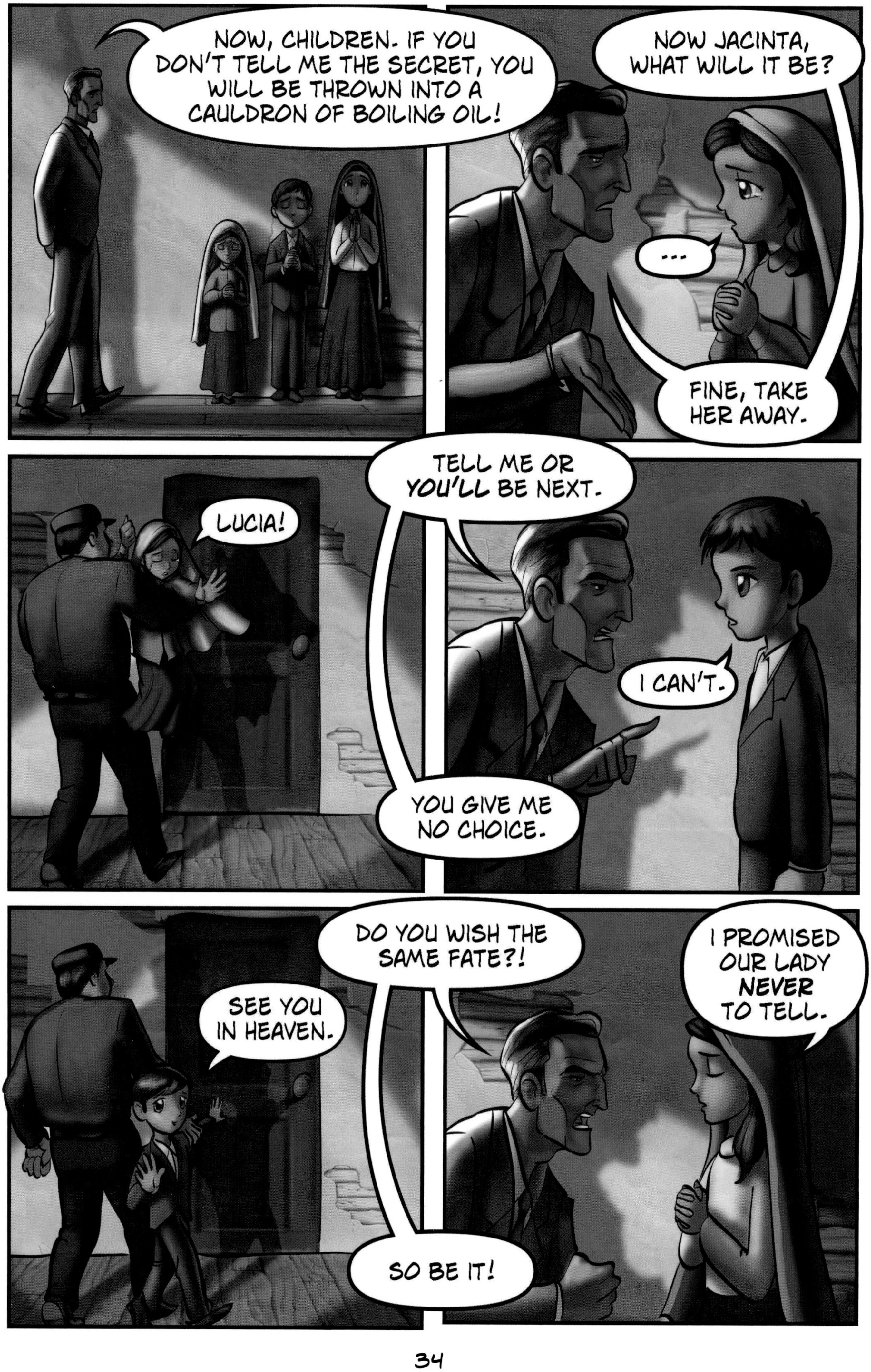
NOW, CHILDREN. IF YOU DON'T TELL ME THE SECRET, YOU WILL BE THROWN INTO A CAULDRON OF BOILING OIL!
NOW JACINTA, WHAT WILL IT BE?
...
FINE, TAKE HER AWAY.
LUCIA!
TELL ME OR YOU'LL BE NEXT.
I CAN'T.
YOU GIVE ME NO CHOICE.
SEE YOU IN HEAVEN.
DO YOU WISH THE SAME FATE?!
SO BE IT!
I PROMISED OUR LADY NEVER TO TELL.

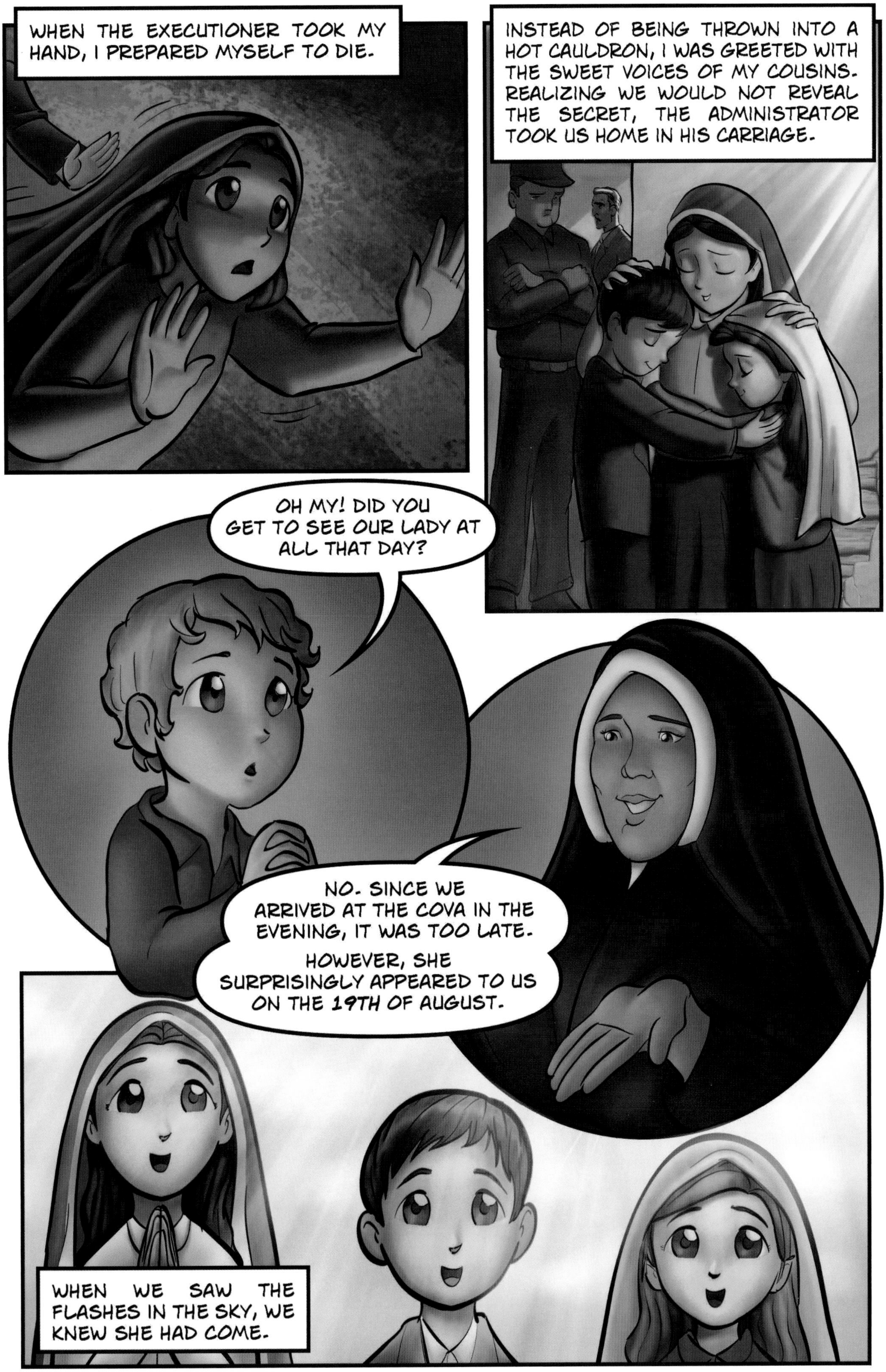
WHEN THE EXECUTIONER TOOK MY HAND, I PREPARED MYSELF TO DIE.
INSTEAD OF BEING THROWN INTO A HOT CAULDRON, I WAS GREETED WITH THE SWEET VOICES OF MY COUSINS. REALIZING WE WOULD NOT REVEAL THE SECRET, THE ADMINISTRATOR TOOK US HOME IN HIS CARRIAGE.
OH MY! DID YOU GET TO SEE OUR LADY AT ALL THAT DAY?
NO. SINCE WE ARRIVED AT THE COVA IN THE EVENING, IT WAS TOO LATE.
HOWEVER, SHE SURPRISINGLY APPEARED TO US ON THE 19TH OF AUGUST.
WHEN WE SAW THE FLASHES IN THE SKY, WE KNEW SHE HAD COME.

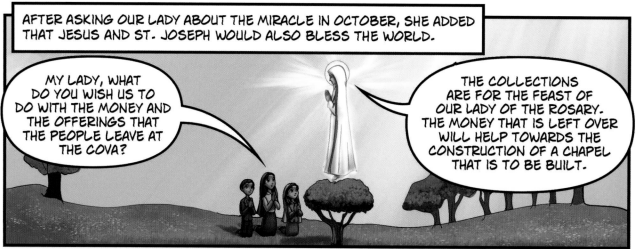

AFTER ASKING OUR LADY ABOUT THE MIRACLE IN OCTOBER, SHE ADDED THAT JESUS AND ST. JOSEPH WOULD ALSO BLESS THE WORLD.

MY LADY, WHAT DO YOU WISH US TO DO WITH THE MONEY AND THE OFFERINGS THAT THE PEOPLE LEAVE AT THE COVA?

THE COLLECTIONS ARE FOR THE FEAST OF OUR LADY OF THE ROSARY. THE MONEY THAT IS LEFT OVER WILL HELP TOWARDS THE CONSTRUCTION OF A CHAPEL THAT IS TO BE BUILT.

LATER, I ASKED IF SHE WOULD HELP CURE THE SICK WHO ASKED FOR PRAYERS. ALTHOUGH SHE PROMISED TO CURE THEM, OUR LADY WAS MORE CONCERNED WITH THEIR SOULS THAN WITH THEIR BODIES.

PRAY! PRAY A GREAT DEAL AND MAKE SACRIFICES FOR SINNERS.

MANY SOULS GO TO HELL FOR NO ONE PRAYS AND OFFERS SACRIFICES FOR THEM.

EVEN AFTER SHE DEPARTED, I COULD STILL HEAR THE WORDS OF OUR LADY RINGING IN MY EARS.

WE HAD AN EVEN STRONGER DESIRE FOR MORTIFICATION, PRAYER AND SUFFERING. WE WISHED TO CLOSE THAT TERRIFYING FURNACE OF HELL SO THAT NO MORE SOULS COULD GO.

September 13, 1917

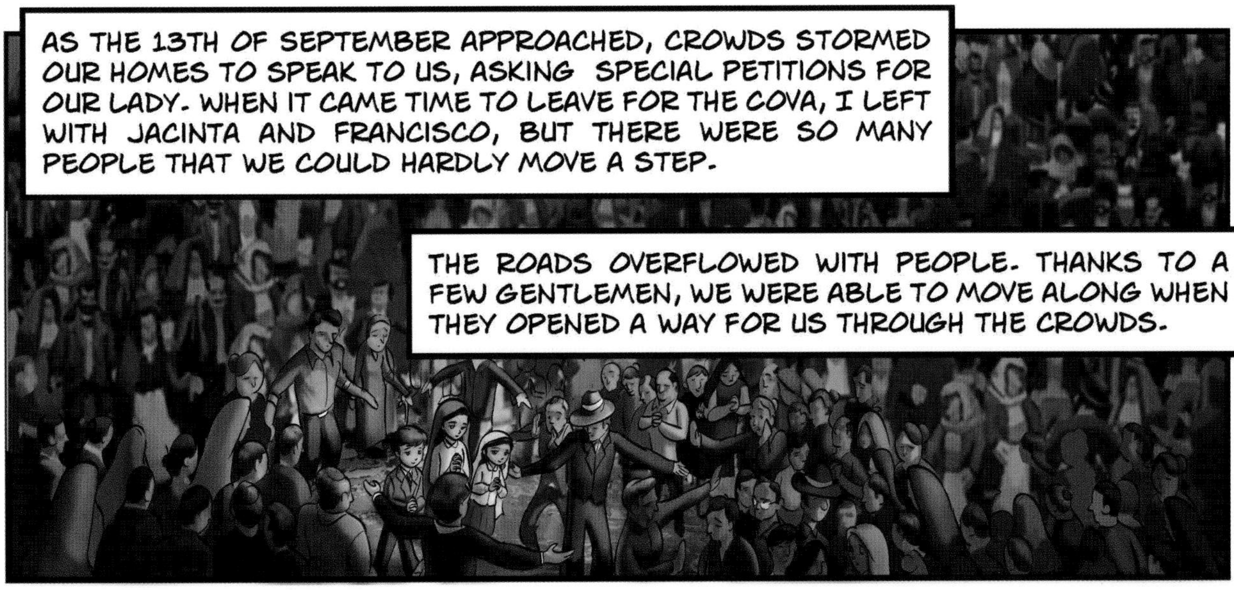
AS THE 13TH OF SEPTEMBER APPROACHED, CROWDS STORMED OUR HOMES TO SPEAK TO US, ASKING SPECIAL PETITIONS FOR OUR LADY. WHEN IT CAME TIME TO LEAVE FOR THE COVA, I LEFT WITH JACINTA AND FRANCISCO, BUT THERE WERE SO MANY PEOPLE THAT WE COULD HARDLY MOVE A STEP.
THE ROADS OVERFLOWED WITH PEOPLE. THANKS TO A FEW GENTLEMEN, WE WERE ABLE TO MOVE ALONG WHEN THEY OPENED A WAY FOR US THROUGH THE CROWDS.

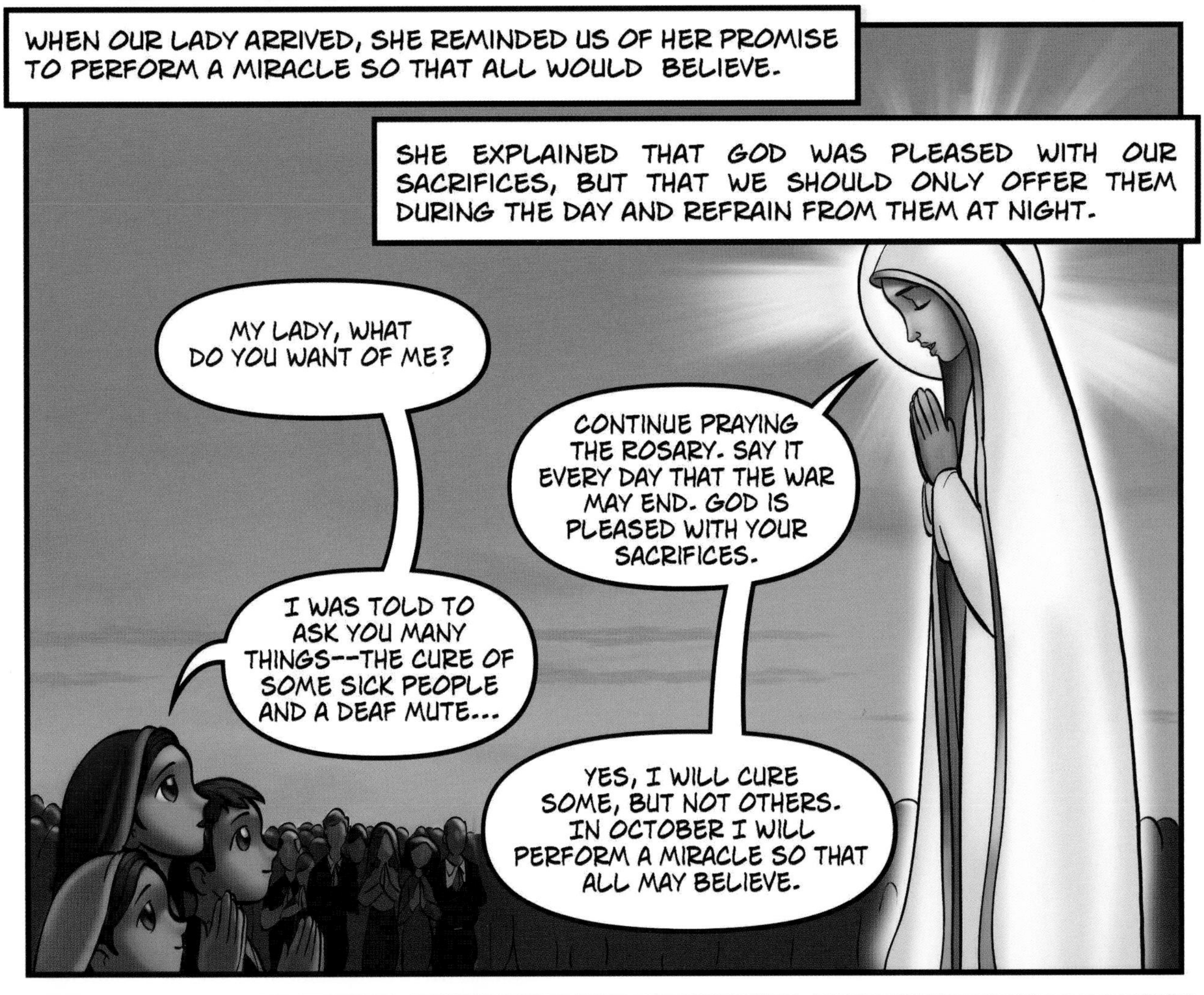
WHEN OUR LADY ARRIVED, SHE REMINDED US OF HER PROMISE TO PERFORM A MIRACLE SO THAT ALL WOULD BELIEVE.
SHE EXPLAINED THAT GOD WAS PLEASED WITH OUR SACRIFICES, BUT THAT WE SHOULD ONLY OFFER THEM DURING THE DAY AND REFRAIN FROM THEM AT NIGHT.
MY LADY, WHAT DO YOU WANT OF ME?
CONTINUE PRAYING THE ROSARY. SAY IT EVERY DAY THAT THE WAR MAY END. GOD IS PLEASED WITH YOUR SACRIFICES.
I WAS TOLD TO ASK YOU MANY THINGS--THE CURE OF SOME SICK PEOPLE AND A DEAF MUTE...
YES, I WILL CURE SOME, BUT NOT OTHERS. IN OCTOBER I WILL PERFORM A MIRACLE SO THAT ALL MAY BELIEVE.

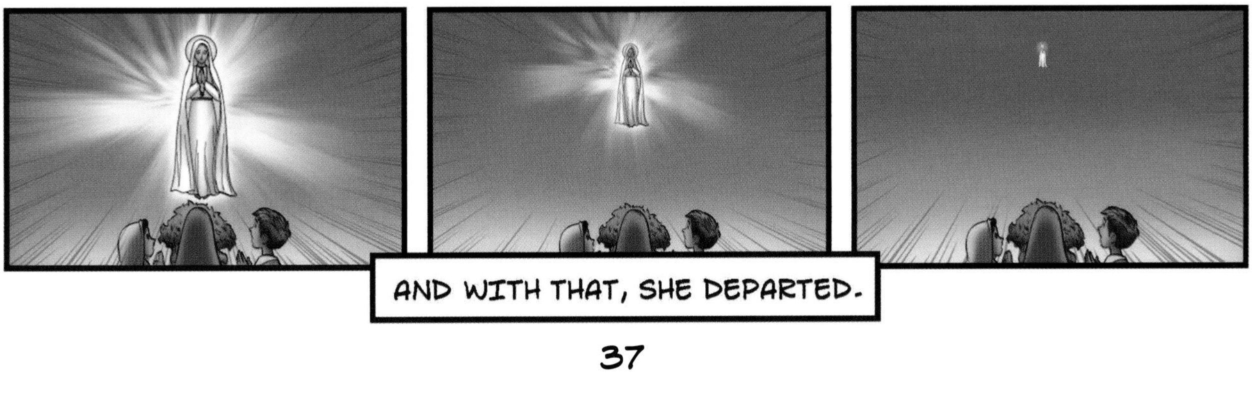
AND WITH THAT, SHE DEPARTED.

NOW, BEFORE WE CONTINUE WITH THE LAST APPARITION, CAN YOU TELL ME A SHORT SUMMARY OF THE MESSAGES?
LET'S SEE. IN 1916, THE ANGEL OF PEACE APPEARED THREE TIMES AND SPOKE OF EUCHARISTIC ADORATION.
ON MAY 13, 1917, OUR LADY ASKED FOR DAILY ROSARIES FOR PEACE IN THE WORLD AND THE END OF THE WAR.
ON JUNE 13, OUR LADY TOLD THE CHILDREN THAT GOD WISHED TO ESTABLISH IN THE WORLD DEVOTION TO HER IMMACULATE HEART.
OH...AND SHE TAUGHT THE "OH MY JESUS" PRAYER IN THE ROSARY!
ON JULY 13, OUR LADY SHOWED THE VISION OF HELL.
ON AUGUST 19, OUR LADY SAID THAT MANY SOULS GO TO HELL, BECAUSE NO ONE IS WILLING TO OFFER SACRIFICES FOR THEM.
ON SEPTEMBER 13, OUR LADY ASKED FOR THE DONATIONS TO BE DEDICATED FOR THE BUILDING OF A CHAPEL.
!?!
WHAT CAN I SAY? YOU'RE A GREAT STORY-TELLER!
I'M SO EXCITED TO HEAR ABOUT THE 13TH OF OCTOBER!
WELL, THE MORNING OF OCTOBER 13 WAS FULL OF HEAVY RAINFALL. NEVERTHELESS, PEOPLE CAME FROM FAR AND WIDE TO WITNESS THE EVENT PROMISED BY OUR LADY. ABOUT 70,000 PEOPLE ALTOGETHER!

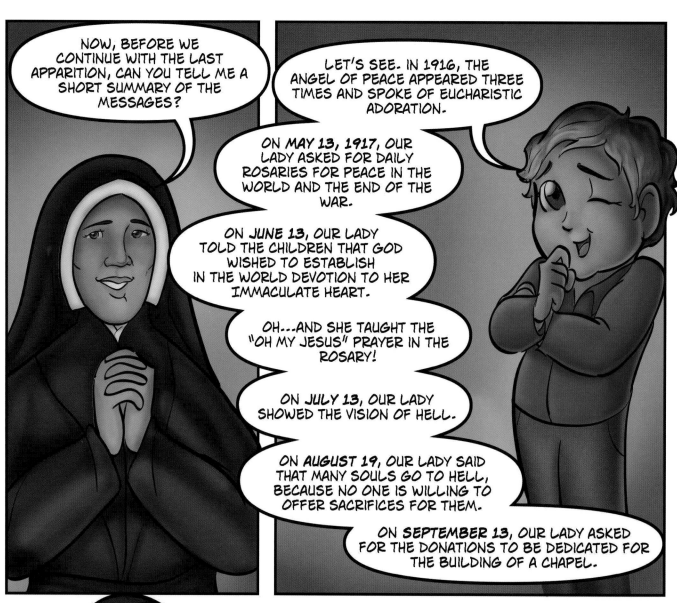

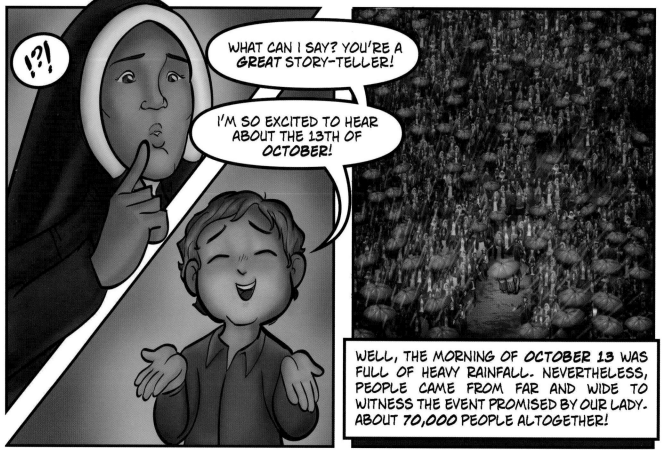

October 13, 1917

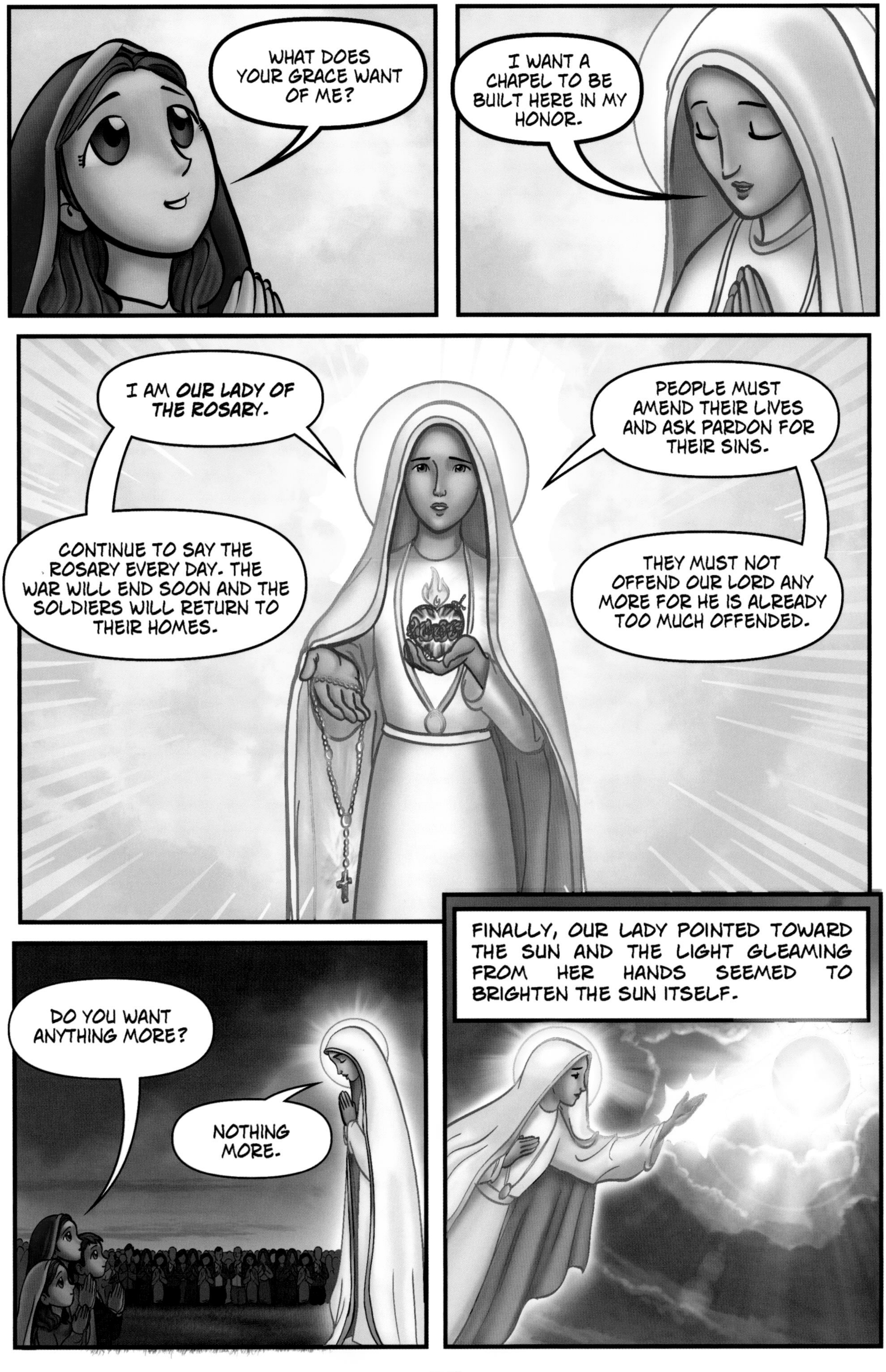
WHAT DOES YOUR GRACE WANT OF ME?
I WANT A CHAPEL TO BE BUILT HERE IN MY HONOR.
I AM OUR LADY OF THE ROSARY.
CONTINUE TO SAY THE ROSARY EVERY DAY. THE WAR WILL END SOON AND THE SOLDIERS WILL RETURN TO THEIR HOMES.
PEOPLE MUST AMEND THEIR LIVES AND ASK PARDON FOR THEIR SINS.
THEY MUST NOT OFFEND OUR LORD ANY MORE FOR HE IS ALREADY TOO MUCH OFFENDED.
DO YOU WANT ANYTHING MORE?
NOTHING MORE.
FINALLY, OUR LADY POINTED TOWARD THE SUN AND THE LIGHT GLEAMING FROM HER HANDS SEEMED TO BRIGHTEN THE SUN ITSELF.

IT WAS AT THIS PRECISE MOMENT THAT THE CLOUDS WERE QUICKLY DISPERSED AND THE SKY WAS CLEAR. THE SUN WAS NOW AS PALE AS THE MOON.

TO THE LEFT OF THE SUN, SAINT JOSEPH APPEARED HOLDING IN HIS LEFT ARM THE CHILD JESUS AS THEY BLESSED THE WORLD.

OUR LADY APPEARED TO THE RIGHT OF THE SUN, DRESSED IN THE BLUE AND WHITE ROBES OF OUR LADY OF THE ROSARY.

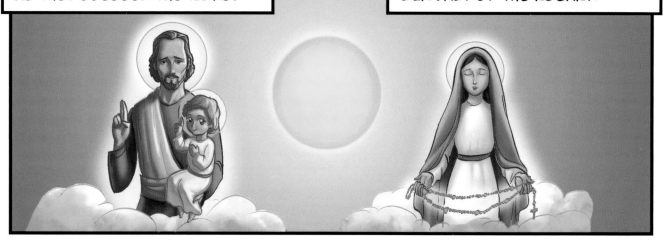

THEN I SAW OUR LORD DRESSED IN RED AS THE DIVINE REDEEMER, BLESSING THE WORLD, AS OUR LADY HAD FORETOLD.

BESIDE HIM STOOD OUR LADY, DRESSED NOW IN THE PURPLE ROBES OF OUR LADY OF SORROWS.

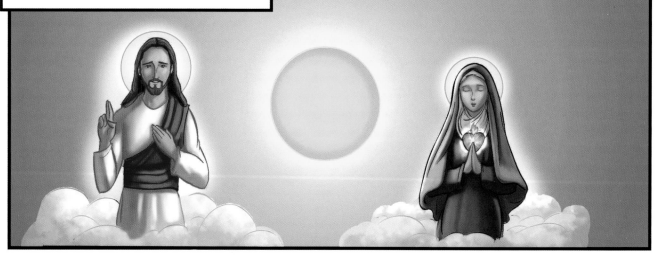

THE BLESSED VIRGIN APPEARED AGAIN IN ALL HER BRIGHTNESS, CLOTHED IN THE SIMPLE BROWN ROBES OF MOUNT CARMEL.

FINALLY, WE ALL WITNESSED THE *MIRACLE OF THE SUN.*

LOOK AT THE SUN!

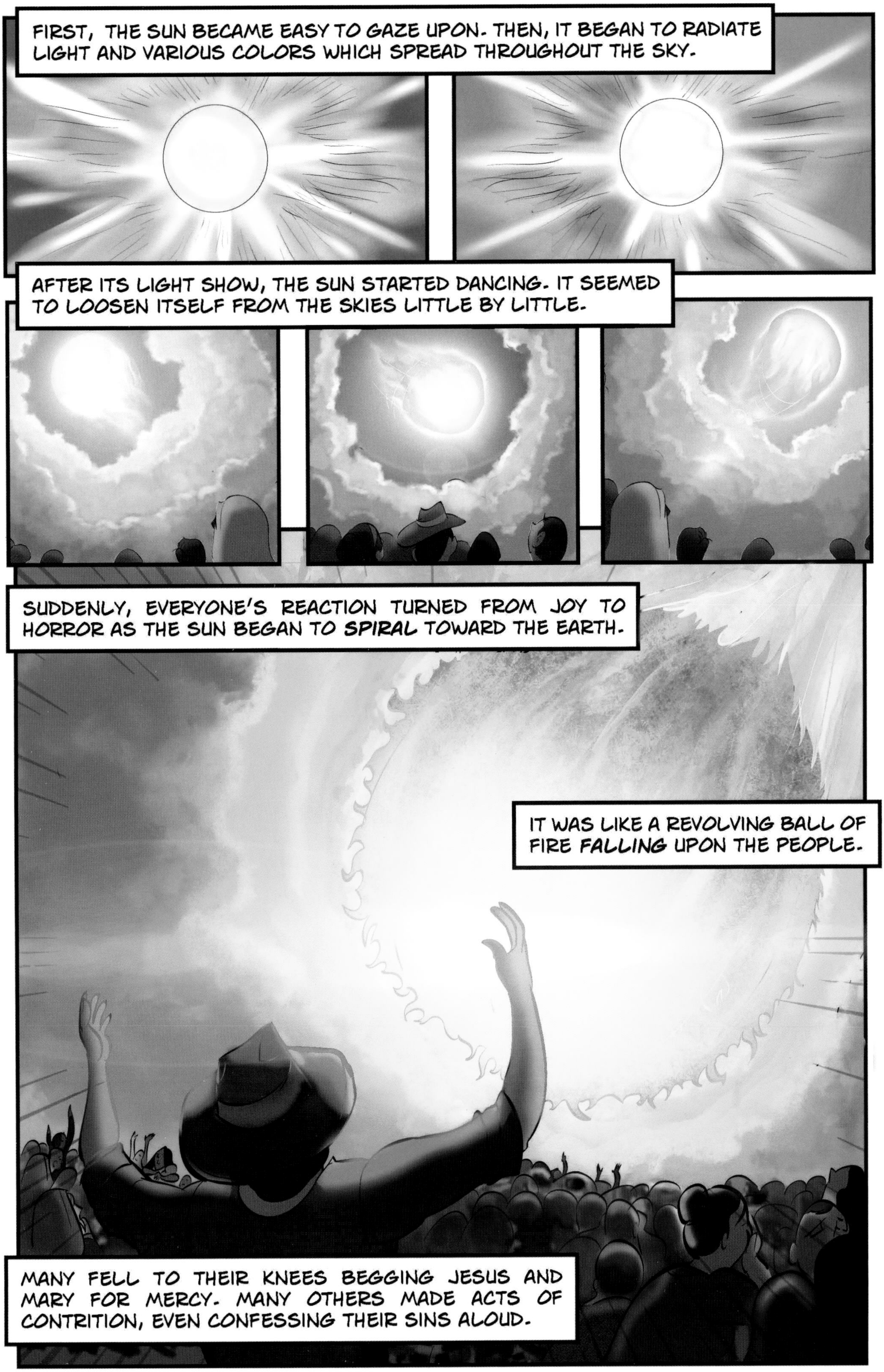
FIRST, THE SUN BECAME EASY TO GAZE UPON. THEN, IT BEGAN TO RADIATE LIGHT AND VARIOUS COLORS WHICH SPREAD THROUGHOUT THE SKY.
AFTER ITS LIGHT SHOW, THE SUN STARTED DANCING. IT SEEMED TO LOOSEN ITSELF FROM THE SKIES LITTLE BY LITTLE.
SUDDENLY, EVERYONE'S REACTION TURNED FROM JOY TO HORROR AS THE SUN BEGAN TO SPIRAL TOWARD THE EARTH.
IT WAS LIKE A REVOLVING BALL OF FIRE FALLING UPON THE PEOPLE.
MANY FELL TO THEIR KNEES BEGGING JESUS AND MARY FOR MERCY. MANY OTHERS MADE ACTS OF CONTRITION, EVEN CONFESSING THEIR SINS ALOUD.

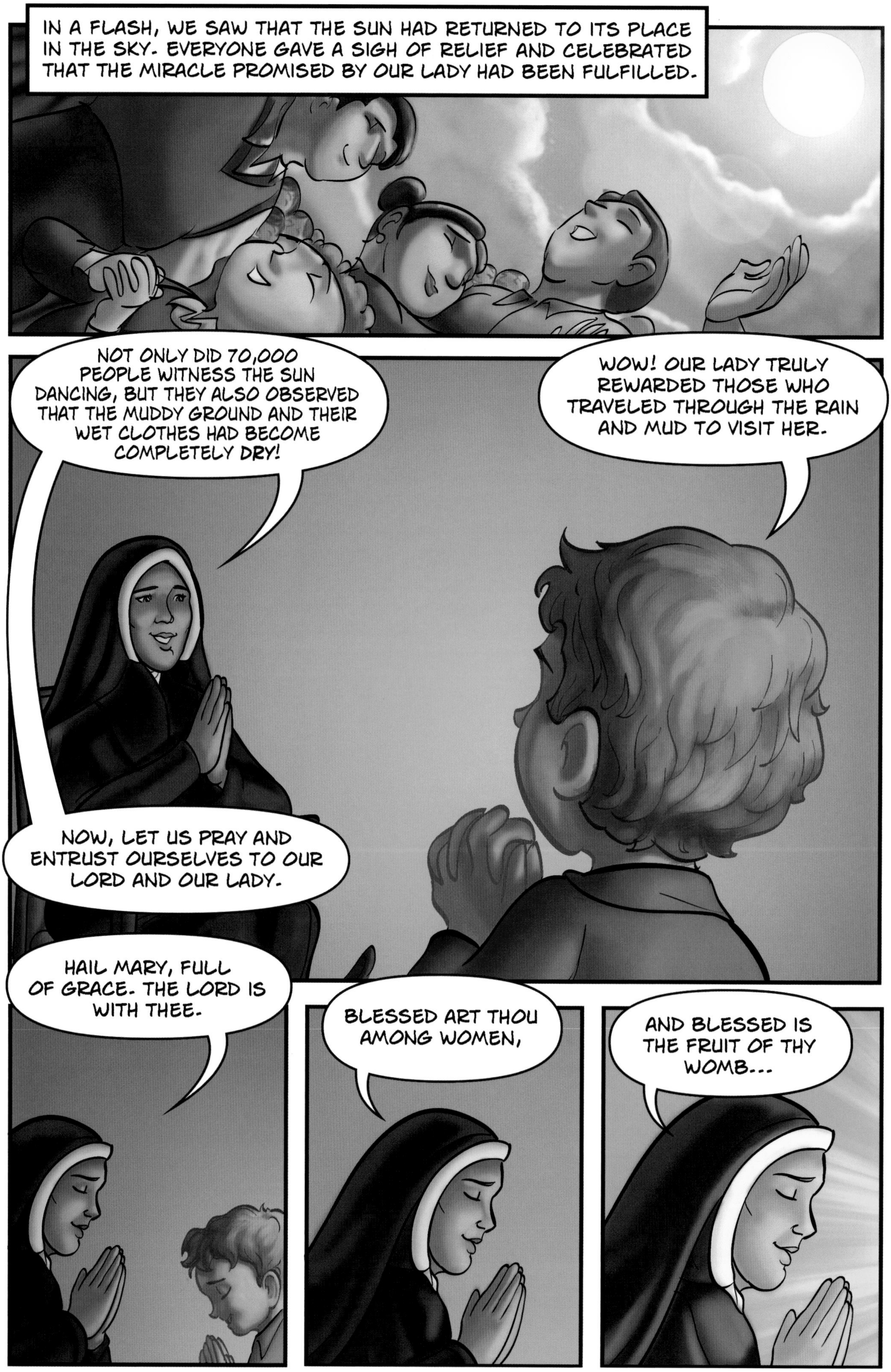
IN A FLASH, WE SAW THAT THE SUN HAD RETURNED TO ITS PLACE IN THE SKY. EVERYONE GAVE A SIGH OF RELIEF AND CELEBRATED THAT THE MIRACLE PROMISED BY OUR LADY HAD BEEN FULFILLED.
NOT ONLY DID 70,000 PEOPLE WITNESS THE SUN DANCING, BUT THEY ALSO OBSERVED THAT THE MUDDY GROUND AND THEIR WET CLOTHES HAD BECOME COMPLETELY DRY!
WOW! OUR LADY TRULY REWARDED THOSE WHO TRAVELED THROUGH THE RAIN AND MUD TO VISIT HER.
NOW, LET US PRAY AND ENTRUST OURSELVES TO OUR LORD AND OUR LADY.
HAIL MARY, FULL OF GRACE. THE LORD IS WITH THEE.
BLESSED ART THOU AMONG WOMEN,
AND BLESSED IS THE FRUIT OF THY WOMB...

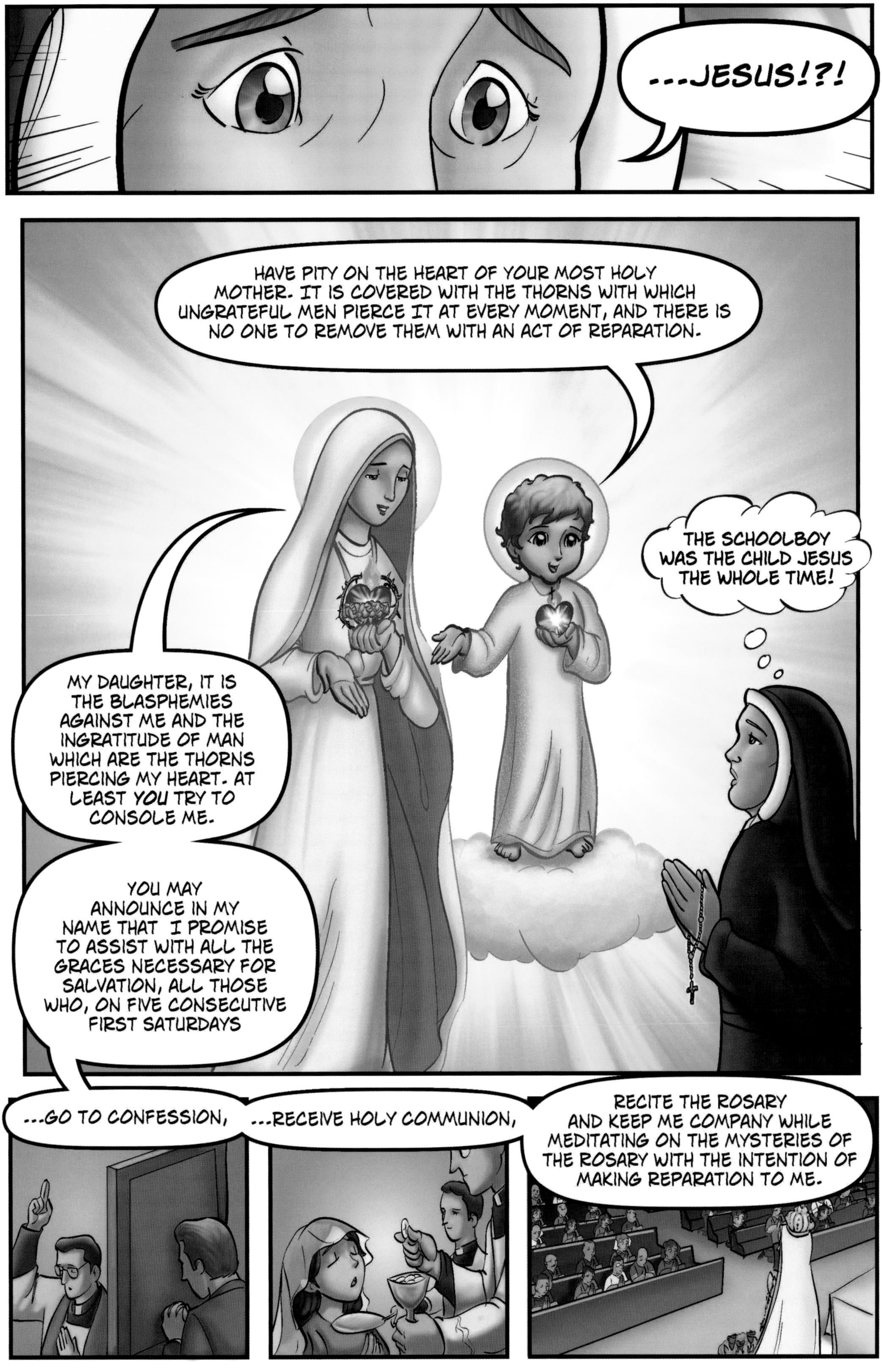
...JESUS!?!
HAVE PITY ON THE HEART OF YOUR MOST HOLY MOTHER. IT IS COVERED WITH THE THORNS WITH WHICH UNGRATEFUL MEN PIERCE IT AT EVERY MOMENT, AND THERE IS NO ONE TO REMOVE THEM WITH AN ACT OF REPARATION.
THE SCHOOLBOY WAS THE CHILD JESUS THE WHOLE TIME!
MY DAUGHTER, IT IS THE BLASPHEMIES AGAINST ME AND THE INGRATITUDE OF MAN WHICH ARE THE THORNS PIERCING MY HEART. AT LEAST YOU TRY TO CONSOLE ME.
YOU MAY ANNOUNCE IN MY NAME THAT I PROMISE TO ASSIST WITH ALL THE GRACES NECESSARY FOR SALVATION, ALL THOSE WHO, ON FIVE CONSECUTIVE FIRST SATURDAYS
...GO TO CONFESSION,
...RECEIVE HOLY COMMUNION,
RECITE THE ROSARY AND KEEP ME COMPANY WHILE MEDITATING ON THE MYSTERIES OF THE ROSARY WITH THE INTENTION OF MAKING REPARATION TO ME.

December 10, 1925

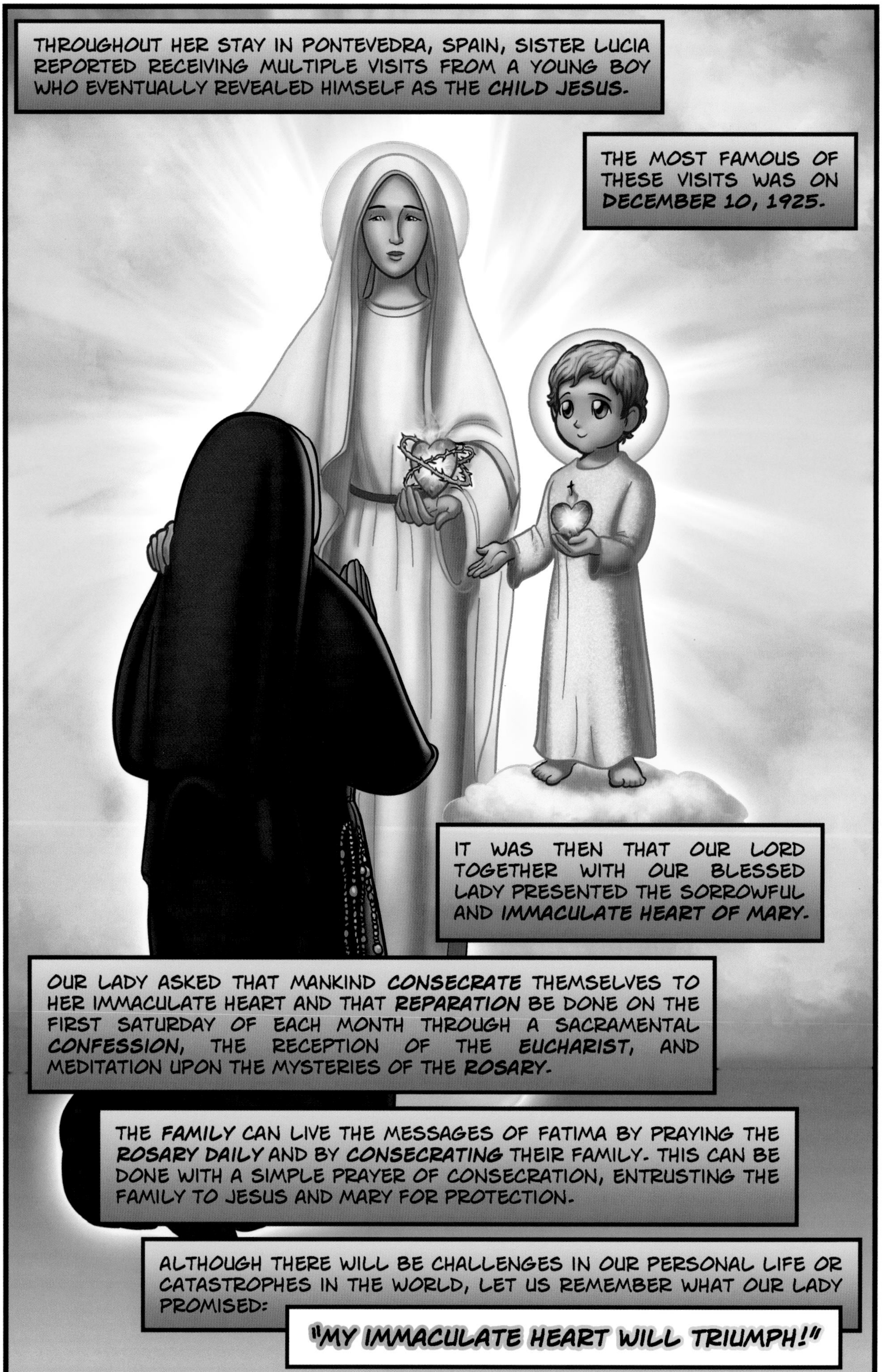
THROUGHOUT HER STAY IN PONTEVEDRA, SPAIN, SISTER LUCIA REPORTED RECEIVING MULTIPLE VISITS FROM A YOUNG BOY WHO EVENTUALLY REVEALED HIMSELF AS THE CHILD JESUS.
THE MOST FAMOUS OF THESE VISITS WAS ON DECEMBER 10, 1925.
IT WAS THEN THAT OUR LORD TOGETHER WITH OUR BLESSED LADY PRESENTED THE SORROWFUL AND IMMACULATE HEART OF MARY.
OUR LADY ASKED THAT MANKIND CONSECRATE THEMSELVES TO HER IMMACULATE HEART AND THAT REPARATION BE DONE ON THE FIRST SATURDAY OF EACH MONTH THROUGH A SACRAMENTAL CONFESSION, THE RECEPTION OF THE EUCHARIST, AND MEDITATION UPON THE MYSTERIES OF THE ROSARY.
THE FAMILY CAN LIVE THE MESSAGES OF FATIMA BY PRAYING THE ROSARY DAILY AND BY CONSECRATING THEIR FAMILY. THIS CAN BE DONE WITH A SIMPLE PRAYER OF CONSECRATION, ENTRUSTING THE FAMILY TO JESUS AND MARY FOR PROTECTION.
ALTHOUGH THERE WILL BE CHALLENGES IN OUR PERSONAL LIFE OR CATASTROPHES IN THE WORLD, LET US REMEMBER WHAT OUR LADY PROMISED:
"MY IMMACULATE HEART WILL TRIUMPH!"

"The Family that prays together stays together." -Fr. Patrick Peyton

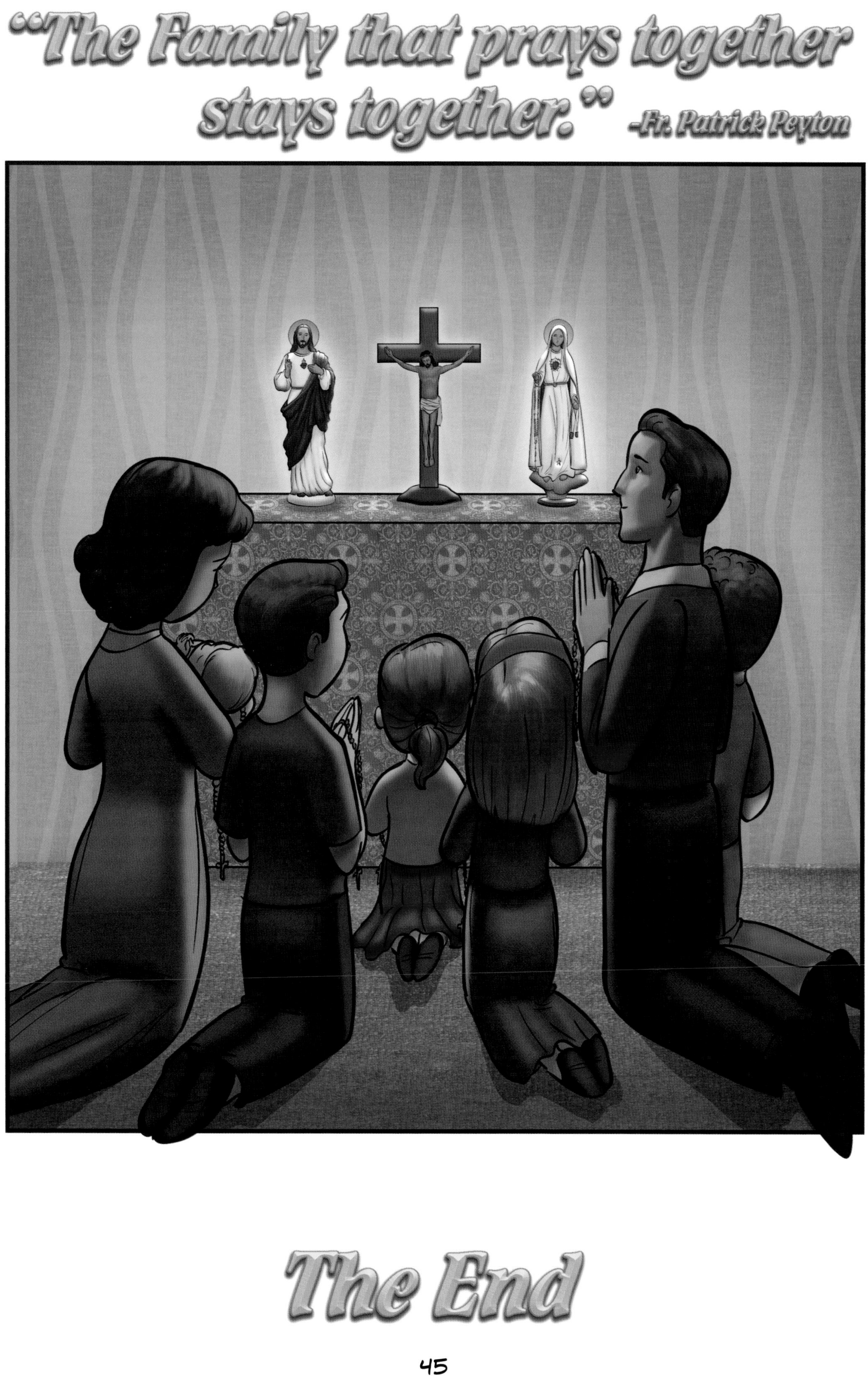

The End

Saint Francisco Marto

(June 11, 1908 – April 4, 1919)

Francisco Marto was the sixth of seven children of Manuel and Olimpia Marto. He was a handsome boy, with light hair and dark eyes. Before the apparitions of Our Lady, he loved to play games with his friends. He played a reed pipe, to which Lucia and his sister Jacinta would sing and dance. He was a kind, gentle boy who always put others first.

During the visits of Our Lady, Francisco saw her, but was not able to hear Our Lady's words. This meant that Lucia had to repeat everything to him, which he often had difficulty understanding as he had not yet learned his catechism. After May 13, 1917, Francisco was never the same. When told that he would go to heaven on the condition that he prayed many rosaries, Francisco said, "I'll pray as many rosaries as you want!"

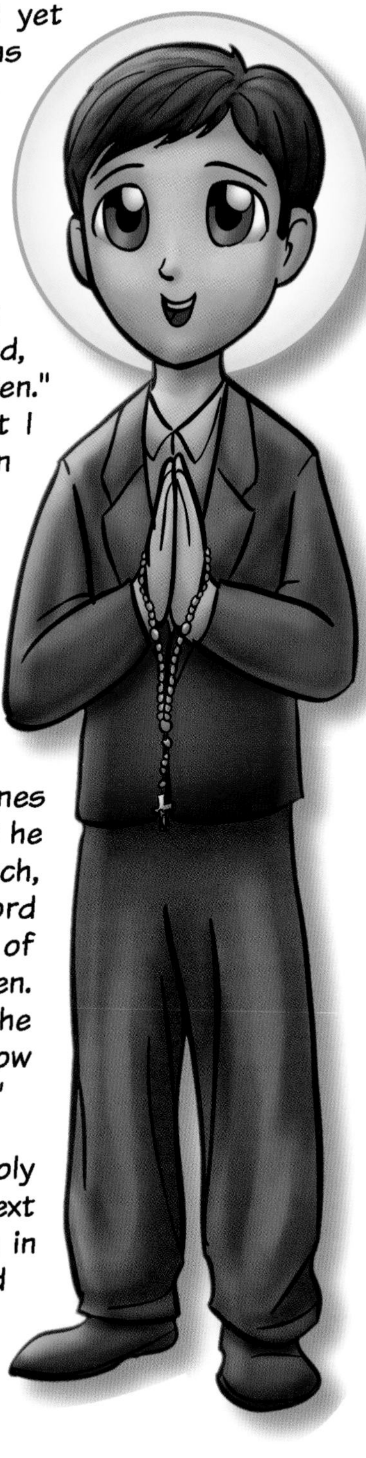

After the apparitions ended, Francisco was enrolled in school, yet he preferred to spend time praying in the church, adoring Jesus in the Tabernacle. When asked what he wanted to be when he grew up, Francisco answered, "I don't want to be anything. I want to die and go to heaven." After the apparitions in 1917, Francisco revealed, "What I liked best about the apparitions was seeing Our Lord in that light that the Blessed Virgin put into our hearts. I love God very much. He is so sad because of so many sins. We must not commit even the smallest sin." His greatest concern was to console the Sacred Heart of Jesus and the Immaculate Heart of His Mother.

In August 1918, when World War I was nearing an end, Francisco and Jacinta both contracted influenza. Without complaint, Francisco took all the medicines prescribed for his sickness, yet assured his family that he would soon die. When Lucia asked if he was suffering much, he replied, "Yes, I am. I suffer it all for the love of Our Lord and Our Lady. I want to suffer more and I can't." On one of his last appeals to Lucia, he said "I'm going soon to Heaven. Jacinta is going to pray a great deal for sinners and for the Holy Father and for you. You're going to stay here below because Our Lady wants you to. Do whatever She wants."

In April of the following year, Francisco asked to receive Holy Communion for the first time and passed away the next morning. He is buried in the Sanctuary at Cova da Iria in Portugal. He was beatified on May 13, 2000 and canonized on May 13, 2017.

St. Francisco, pray for us!

Saint Jacinta Marto

(March 11, 1910 – February 20, 1920)

Jacinta de Jesus Marto was the youngest child of Manuel and Olimpia Marto's seven children. She had a sweet singing voice and a gift for dancing. Before the Fatima apparitions Jacinta was quite affectionate, but would pout when she did not get her way.

After the Blessed Virgin showed the children a vision of hell, Jacinta said, "We must make many, many sacrifices and pray a lot for sinners so that no one shall ever again have to go to that prison of fire where people suffer so much." Wishing that souls would be converted, she would tell Lucia, "If only I could place in the heart of everyone the fire which I have in my heart which makes me love the Heart of Mary so much!"

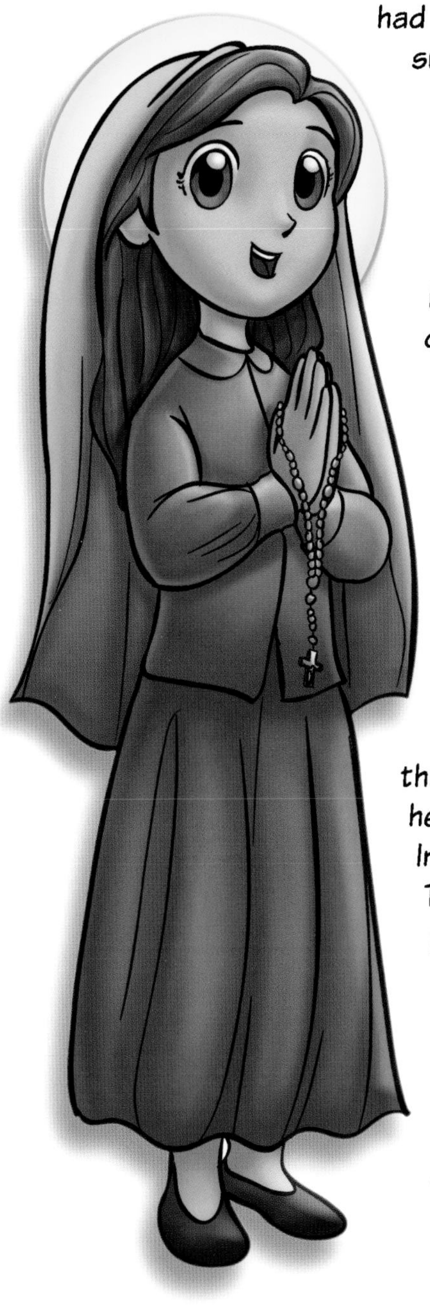

In her biography, Sister Lúcia said that Jacinta had told her of having had many personal visions after 1917. After seeing a vision of a suffering pope, Jacinta said, "Poor Holy Father, I feel much pity for sinners!" From that time on, Christ's Vicar was always present in her prayers and sacrifices. When shown the reality of sin, she reported, "The sins of the world are too great. If only people knew what eternity is, they would do everything to change their lives. People lose their souls because they do not think about the death of Our Lord and do not do penance."

In 1918, she and her brother Francisco both became ill. Despite their illness, Jacinta and Francisco continued to walk to church, prostrating themselves in prayer for hours as the Angel of Peace had instructed them to do. Even when her sickness worsened and she became bed-ridden, Jacinta cheerfully declared that her sufferings were just opportunities to offer for the conversion of sinners. She even motivated her older cousin Lucia to evangelize, saying "Don't go and hide. Tell everyone that God grants us graces through the Immaculate Heart of Mary; that people are to ask her for them; and that the Heart of Jesus wants the Immaculate Heart of Mary to be venerated at his side. Tell them also to pray to the Immaculate Heart of Mary for peace, since God entrusted it to her."

Finally, on the night of February 20, 1920, she joined her brother in eternity. Jacinta and Francisco were beatified on May 13, 2000 and canonized on May 13, 2017. They are the Catholic Church's youngest canonized saints, who did not die as martyrs.

St. Jacinta, pray for us!

Sister Lucia dos Santos

(March 22, 1907 – February 13, 2005)

Lucia was the daughter of Antonio and Maria Rosa dos Santos and the youngest of seven children. At the age of eight, she was responsible for tending the family's sheep, often accompanied by her cousins. She was known for her leadership qualities, often organizing games, dances, prayers and other activities for the children of the village. Lucia and her siblings were well-versed in basic Church teaching, having been taught their catechism by her mother.

When Our Lady asked if she and her cousins wanted to offer themselves to God as an act of reparation. Lucia spoke for all of them, saying, "Yes, we do!" Our Lady prophesied that she would suffer a great deal and it was not long before she was accused of lying. Despite the persecution from even her own family, Lucia continued to lead her cousins to the Cova da Iria on the 13th of each month. It was only after the miracle of the sun on October 13, 1917, that everyone truly believed her.

The next year, her cousins fell ill. Lucia remembered what the Blessed Mother had foretold: "I will take Jacinta and Francisco soon. You, however, are to stay here a longer time. Jesus wants to use you to make Me known and loved. He wants to establish the Devotion to My Immaculate Heart in the world." Once her cousins passed away, Lucia's mission began.

After seeking the assistance of the Bishop of Leiria, Fatima, Lucia joined the school of the Dorothean Sisters of Villar in 1921. In 1925, Lucia became a postulant of Saint Dorothy in Spain. It was there that she continued to have visions of Our Lord and Our Lady concerning the consecration of Russia and the message of reparation to the Immaculate Heart of Mary. In 1948, she entered the Carmelite order of Saint Joseph in Coimbra where she took the name of Sister Maria Lucia of the Immaculate Heart. Over the years, Sr. Lucia wrote books recounting the events of Fatima, giving answers to the many questions about how to live the message of the Blessed Mother. Her earthly mission finally came to an end on February 13, 2005 at the age of ninety-seven.

More can be found in her writings: "FATIMA in Lucia's Own Words."